Hooray for the USA!

Written by Loralyn Radcliffe
Illustrations by Ken Tunell
Cover by Denise Bauer

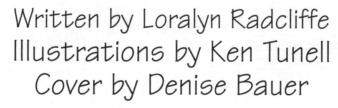

Teacher Created Materials, Inc.

D1275169

Teacher Created Materials, Inc.

6421 Industry Way

Westminster, CA 92683

www.teachercreated.com

© 1999 Teacher Created Materials, Inc.

Reprinted, 2000

Made in U.S.A.

ISBN #1-57690-361-3

Library of Congress Catalog Card Number: 98-061565

Editor:

Marsha Kearns

Table of Contents

Table of Contents *(cont.)*

Introduction

Welcome to Hooray for the USA!

Hey, Kids!

Welcome to *Hooray for the USA!* This book celebrates the United States and us—our holidays and heroes, our monuments and memorials, and our symbols and states. It is packed with ideas for crafts, games, activities, and recipes related to our fascinating country. Invite a parent or friend along as you explore the United States of America.

Dear Adults,

This book is a fun and activity-oriented way for you to help bring history into the present for your child. Through reading, activities, crafts, and cooking, you can discover what really interests your child and use that understanding as a catalyst for digging deeper into a particular topic.

Hooray for the USA! takes a topical approach to American history rather than a chronological sequencing of events. However, to put what you learn into perspective, you may want to make a giant time line on which to record important dates of events and people's lives presented. Be sure to learn about each holiday as it occurs.

Find Out More sections are particularly exciting. Titles of picture books and Web sites are given for extending the topics. Great care has been taken to find Web sites that are fun, interesting, somehow unique, and, of course, appropriate for your child. No dull pages filled only with text! Please be careful to type in the Web addresses carefully and to monitor your child when he or she uses the Internet.

Finally, a note of caution. Please be careful when using tools or materials that are hot, sharp, or otherwise dangerous. Some of the projects need direct and continuous adult supervision, others only a minimal amount. Read through the crafts and recipes before you present them to your child so you can determine the amount of your participation that may be required.

Enjoy your trip through the USA, and have fun sharing it with your child!

How to Use This Book

The informational articles and fun projects in this 160-page book will tie the past into the present for you and your child.

Page through the book to familiarize yourself with the content and crafts so you can choose the appropriate learning activity for the time of year or to suit your and your child's interests.

The projects show artwork so you can easily guide your child, if necessary, toward successful completion of the crafts. Materials are listed, many of which can probably be found in your home. Other items may be easily purchased in hobby shops or grocery stores or found in nature.

Read the brief article that precedes the activity you choose, and talk with your child about them both. Make sure you have the necessary materials for the craft on hand before you begin. Note the projects that will require adult supervision and/or help so that you can allot the necessary time.

The sections in this book are the following:

Holidays
Tie information and activities to the major holidays celebrated in our country.

Heroes
Get to know some of the people of the past and the present who helped make America great.

Symbols
Identify the symbols that stand for the sacrifices, struggles, and successes of Americans.

Monuments and Memorials
Visit some of the magnificent structures that a grateful nation has erected to honor its heroes.

Native Americans
Connect with the first people who lived in our land and celebrate their unique and valuable contributions.

All Around America
Gain a broad overview of our 50 states and their people. Also learn how to search the Web for information on specific states.

Holidays

Presidents' Day

Presidents' Day is celebrated on the third Monday in February. Since their birthdays were both in February, we previously focused on George Washington and Abraham Lincoln on this holiday. Now it serves as a day on which we can remember and honor all the presidents of the United States.

The U.S. Constitution requires that the president be a natural-born citizen of the United States and not younger than 35 years old. The person must have been a resident of the United States for 14 years at the time of inauguration. Thus far, only men have been elected to serve as president. The wife of the president is known as the First Lady.

The president of the United States has a variety of official government duties and responsibilities. He is the Commander in Chief of the U.S. Army, Navy, and Air Force. He meets and visits with foreign dignitaries, which may involve helping negotiate peace treaties, discussing foreign trade policy, or hosting dinners. He has the power to sign or veto bills and laws presented by Congress. He delivers the State of the Union address once a year to let U.S. citizens know how their nation is doing.

The president also has many ceremonial duties, including awarding medals to heroes, laying the wreath on the Tomb of the Unknown Soldier, lighting the White House Christmas tree, and greeting visitors.

Find Out More

. . . in a Book

Money by Joe Cribb (Knopf Books, 1990). This Eyewitness Book has photos and information about money from all over the world.

The President's Cabinet and How It Grew by Nancy Winslow Parker (HarperTrophy, 1991). Who advises the president? Find out how this special group of people works to help the president run the country.

. . . on the Web

http://www.grolier.com/presidents/nbk/quiz/nbkquiz.html—Test your knowledge of the presidents with this 25-question interactive quiz.

http://members.macconnect.com/users/j/jrpotter/puzzles/presidents—Print out a U.S. presidents word search.

Pictures of Presidents on Money

Much of our money has pictures of presidents. On the lines, write the name of the president whose face is on our:

one-dollar bill

_____

five-dollar bill

_____

fifty-dollar bil

_____

quarter

_____

nickel

_____

dime

_____

penny

_____

half dollar

_____

- -

Fold or cover before doing this activity.

Bogus Bucks

What You Need

- ruler
- pencil
- fine-tip black marker
- white paper 8 ½" x 11" (22 cm x 28 cm)
- scissors

What To Do

1. Fold the paper in half lengthwise. Fold it in half lengthwise again.

2. Turn the paper and fold it in half again. The paper should look like a skinny dollar bill.

3. Open the paper. You will have fold lines around eight rectangles.

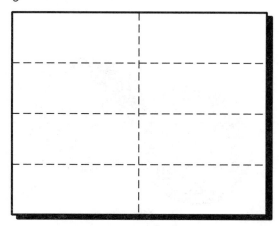

4. Use the ruler and pen to mark straight black lines on the fold lines.

5. In pencil, sketch a picture of yourself and a design on the bills. Show how much the bills are worth.

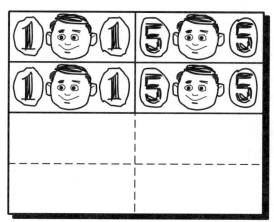

6. Trace over your drawings with the black pen. When the ink is completely dry, erase any stray pencil marks.

7. Cut the bucks apart and pass them out to your friends and family.

Try This

- At a photocopy center, make colored copies of your page of Bogus Bucks.
- Design a backside for your bucks and make two-sided copies.

Penny Shine

What You Need

- tarnished pennies
- 1 cup (250 mL) vinegar
- 1 tablespoon (15 mL) salt
- plastic container

What To Do

1. Put the pennies in the plastic container.

2. Pour the vinegar over the pennies.

3. Put the salt into the vinegar. Wait a few minutes.

4. Drain the clean, shiny pennies and rinse them in clear water.

The Fourth of July

On the United States' Independence Day, the Fourth of July, we celebrate the anniversary of the founding of our democratic nation. Flags are displayed proudly, Uncle Sam leads town parades, patriotic music fills the air, and spectacular fireworks light up the sky.

On July 4, 1776, the United Colonies of America adopted the Declaration of Independence, the document that declares the United States to be "Free and Independent States" and that "all political connection between them and the State of Great Britain, is and ought to be totally dissolved." This document also promised all citizens equal right to "life, liberty, and the pursuit of happiness."

The first Independence Day celebration took place in Philadelphia on July 4, 1777. The Fourth of July remains a grand day of fun, festivity, and rededication to the principles and spirit of democracy.

In England and other countries, soldiers marched to music when they went to battle. The familiar song "Yankee Doodle" was originally written by an Englishman to make fun of colonists because they were not good soldiers. During the Revolutionary War, the colonists adopted the song as their own. Imagine how the British felt when they had to march to "Yankee Doodle" as they surrendered at Yorktown!

Find Out More

. . . in a Book

Yankee Doodle by Steven Kellogg (Four Winds Press, 1976).

Fourth of July on the Plains by Jean Van Leeuwen (Dial Books, 1997).

. . . on the Web

http://www.holidays.net/independence/—Find patriotic music, fireworks, recipe for Mom's apple pie, an Uncle Sam craft, and the Declaration of Independence.

http://www.pbs.org/ktca/liberty/game/index.html—Test your knowledge of the American Revolution by playing The Road to Revolution.

Yankee Doodle Flute

What You Need

- paper towel tube
- pencil
- wax paper
- rubber band
- scissors
- blue or red paint
- star stickers

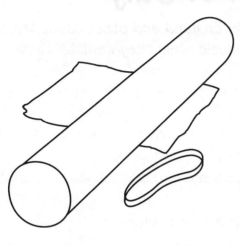

What To Do

1. Paint the outside of the tube with red or blue paint; let dry.

2. Use a sharp pencil to punch four or five holes in a line down the length of the tube.

3. Cut a 3" (8 cm) square of wax paper. Place it over the end of the tube and secure it with the rubber band.

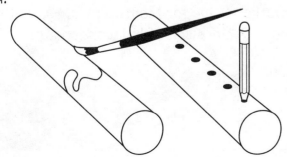

4. Decorate the flute with star stickers.

5. Hum into the open end of the flute and pretend to play by covering the holes with your fingers.

Labor Day

Labor Day is a special holiday that honors working people by giving them a day off of work to rest on the first Monday in September. In the past, the working conditions of many jobs were very poor. Workers sometimes worked 12 to 14 hours a day, six or seven days a week for little pay and in hazardous or unhealthy conditions. At times, even very young children of six or seven had to work 10-hour days to help their families survive.

Unhappy workers joined together to form unions, which united the people in a certain trade. With the power of many people behind them, union representatives were able to negotiate with employers to improve working conditions, pay, and benefits.

The New York Central Labor Union organized the first Labor Day celebration in 1882. The celebration was so successful that several cities organized their own celebrations the following year, and by 1894 Labor Day was a national holiday.

Find Out More

. . . in a Book

Worksong by Gary Paulsen (Harcourt, Brace and Co., 1997). This beautifully illustrated book shows all sorts of people at work.

Job Book

What You Need

- file folder
- white paper
- hole punch
- yarn or ribbon
- pencil, crayons, or markers
- scissors

What To Do

1. Cut the white paper in half.

2. Trim the file folder so that it is slightly larger than the paper. Punch three holes along the fold of the folder.

3. Stack the papers and place them in the folder. Mark on the top one where the folder holes are.

4. Remove the papers and punch the holes where you marked them. Replace the papers inside the folder, lining up the holes.

5. Tie yarn or ribbon loosely through the sets of holes to bind the book.

6. Write your parent's job title, responsibilities, the name of the company, and work phone number.

7. Include a photograph of your parent at work or in his/her work clothes.

8. Describe the job you would like to have when you grow up, and draw a picture of yourself working.

Memorial Day

Memorial Day is celebrated on May 30 or the last Monday in May. This day is set aside to honor those who have been killed in service to our country. Respect is shown for the dead by decorating their graves with flags and flowers. Flower wreaths are used, too. Often there is a parade, and people give speeches.

Memorial Wreath

Make a patriotic wreath for your front door.

What You Need

- paper plate
- red, white, and blue curling ribbon
- red, white, and blue construction paper
- aluminum foil
- scissors
- glue

What To Do

1. Cut out the center of the paper plate, leaving about a 2" (5 cm) rim.

2. Cut different-sized stars from construction paper and foil. Glue them to the wreath.

3. Curl various lengths of the ribbon and glue them on the wreath.

4. Glue a loop of ribbon to use as a hanger onto the back of the plate.

Find Out More

. . . in a Book

In Flanders Fields: The Story of the Poem by John McCrae by Linda Granfield (Delacorte Press, 1995). Beautiful artwork accompanies the famous poem, and brief historical sketches are given of the poet and World War I.

. . . on the Web

http://www.geocities.com/Athens/Acropolis/1465/memorial.html—This interesting site includes graphics, photos, poetry, and links to memorials around the country.

Paper Poppies

What You Need

- red and yellow tissue paper
- green pipe cleaners
- clear tape or green florist's tape
- glue

What To Do

1. Cut the red tissue paper into several 6" (15 cm) circles.

2. Poke a pipe cleaner through the center of the circles until it sticks up through the paper about 1–1½" (2.54 cm–3.8 cm).

3. Bend the top of the pipe cleaner in half and pinch the bent part together to form the flower's stamen, or center.

4. Gather the bottom of the tissue petals around the pipe cleaner until the flower takes shape.

5. Wrap a piece of tape around the tissue and pipe cleaner to hold the flower shape in place.

6. Tear off two or three small pieces of yellow tissue and roll them into balls. Glue them around the stamen.

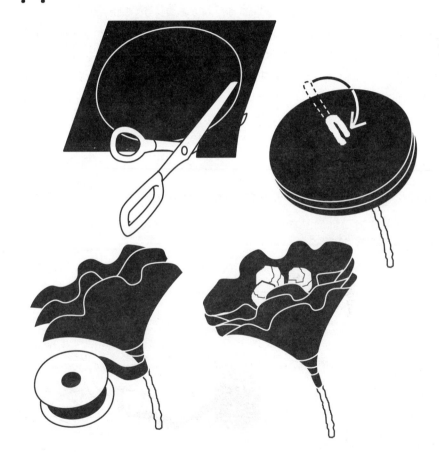

Try This

Stack a 6" (15 cm), 5" (13 cm), and 4" (10 cm) tissue circle together. Use different colors of tissue for each circle, or cut fringes or petal shapes from the different circles.

Martin Luther King, Jr., Day

The Emancipation Proclamation of 1863 gave freedom and equality to the African Americans held as slaves in the United States. Nearly 100 years later, things had not changed enough. In many states whites and blacks remained separate and were treated differently.

Many African Americans struggled—and continue to struggle—for true equality. One of the most courageous was Dr. Martin Luther King, Jr., and his message that goals can be reached with dignity and love through nonviolence still lives today. A wonderful and moving speaker, Dr. King spent his life persuading people to end discrimination. His words and actions motivated millions and caused real change.

Dr. King gave his important and stirring "I Have a Dream" speech at a peaceful demonstration he helped organize in 1963, called the March on Washington.

"I have a dream that one day . . . the sons of former slaves and the sons of former slave owners will be able to sit down together at the table of brotherhood. . . . I have a dream that my four little children will one day live in a nation where they will not be judged by the color of their skin but by the content of their character."

Martin Luther King, Jr., Day

Sadly, not all people shared this belief or dream of equality for all. Martin Luther King, Jr., was killed by an assassin on April 4, 1968. Dr. King was born January 15, 1929. Now, on the third Monday of January each year, the people of the United States honor him for his courage, his words, and his dream.

Find Out More

. . . in a Book

Martin Luther King by Malcah Zeldis and Rosemary L. Bray (Greenwillow, 1995). This biography features fabulous paintings of Dr. King's life.

Whoever You Are by Mem Fox (Harcourt, Brace and Co., 1997) This beautiful book shows that children are the same the world over, no matter what the color of their skin.

Dinner at Aunt Connie's House by Faith Ringgold (Hyperion, 1993, 1996). Twelve courageous African American women talk about their lives.

My Dream of Martin Luther King by Faith Ringgold (Crown Publishing Group, 1996).

. . . on the Web

http://www.Webcorp.com/civilrights/mlk.htm—Listen to audio clips from Dr. King's "I Have a Dream" speech.

http://daycare.miningco.com/library/weekly/bljan19th.htm —Print out a coloring page of Dr. King or a black history word search.

Columbus Day

Late in the fifteenth century, Italian explorer Christopher Columbus approached King Ferdinand and Queen Isabella of Spain with a plan to get gold and spices from India. These riches had previously been brought to Europe by costly overland caravans. Columbus reasoned that if he kept sailing west he would eventually reach Asia by boat. Ferdinand and Isabella agreed to finance the trip and promised Columbus honors and a percentage of the trade resulting from this new sea route to Asia.

In 1492, after three weeks at sea, Columbus mistakenly landed in North America. For hundreds of years Columbus was credited with discovering America. We now know that other Europeans such as Leif Ericson arrived well before Columbus. Although he never found the route he was looking for, Columbus did open the New World to further European exploration and eventual settlement.

The second Monday of October is recognized as Columbus Day. In spite of differing feelings about honoring the "wrong" discoverer, our government still acknowledges Christopher Columbus's incredible voyage on three small ships named the Niña, the Pinta, and the Santa Maria.

Find Out More

. . . in a Book

The Encounter by Jane Yolen (Harcourt, Brace and Co., 1992). This book tells about Columbus's explorations from the viewpoint of a young boy.

. . . on the Web

http://www.lofthouse.com/Christopher/preview/index.html —See photos and listen to sound clips from "Christopher: The Musical of Discovery."

Sailboat

What You Need

- empty plastic bottle with cap
- sand
- pencil
- scissors
- paper

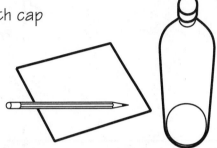

What To Do

1. Put enough sand in the bottle to keep it stable in water. Put on the cap and shake the sand so it is evenly distributed on the bottom of the bottle.

2. With the bottle laying sideways, sand on the bottom, use scissors to carefully poke a hole large enough to insert a pencil as a mast.

3. Design and cut out a sail. Tape it to the mast.

4. Float your boat!

Try This

Make several boats and race them in a small basin of water. Baby bathtubs work well for this.

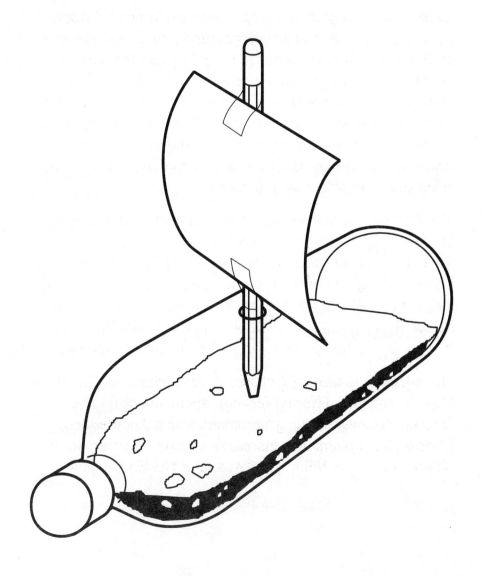

Paper Boat

What You Need

- construction or copy paper
- 2 pennies

What To Do

1. Lay the paper horizontally and fold it in half.

2. Open the paper and fold the top and bottom sides until the edges meet at the center fold. Make sure the edges touch but do not overlap.

3. Turn the paper upside down

4. Fold the four corners in to the center fold.

5. Fold the paper in half lengthwise.

6. Pull the layers apart at the top by opening two layers to one side and one layer to the other side.

7. Fold the points in and crease them. Then press on the bottom to form the shape of the boat.
   Turn the boat over and use your thumb to crease the seams at both ends.

8. Round out the boat and raise the sides to complete.

Note: If your boat lists or tips, put one or two pennies in the boat to balance it in the water.

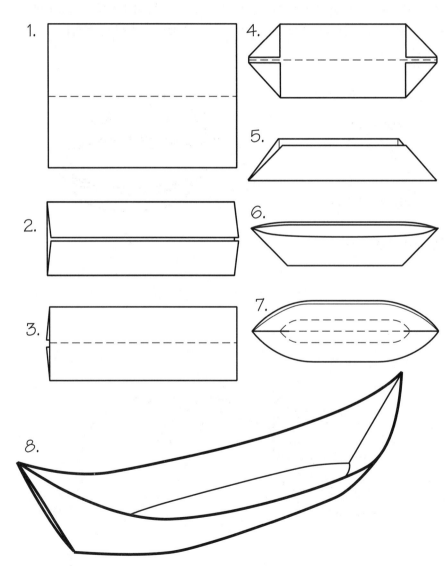

Compass

A compass is a magnet that is attracted to the nearest magnetic poles of the Earth. A compass helps find direction.

What You Need

- sewing needle
- magnet
- cork
- pan of water

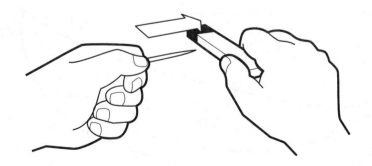

What To Do

1. Hold one end of the needle and stroke the other end in ONE DIRECTION ONLY with the magnet. (Don't rub the needle back and forth.)

2. Float the cork in the pan of water.

3. Place the magnetized needle on the cork. The cork will move until the magnetized end of the needle points north.

Try This

Use different types of magnets such as bar or horseshoe. Find out what what they will attract and what they will repel.

Veterans Day

Veterans Day, celebrated on November 11, honors all the men and women who have ever served our country in the United States armed forces.

Originally, this holiday was called Armistice Day. It commemorated the truce made November 11, 1918, that ended World War I—the "War to End All Wars."

November 11 was declared a federal holiday in 1938, but shortly thereafter peace was shattered by the beginning of World War II.

In 1954, Congress changed the name of the holiday to Veterans Day in order to better honor all veterans. People remember this holiday with celebrations, parades, speeches, and special services.

Find Out More

. . . in a Book

The Wall by Eve Bunting (Clarion, 1990).

. . . on the Web

http://www.geocities.com/Athens/Acropolis/1465/vets.html—This site features poetry, graphics, and many links to the various branches of the armed forces.

Army

Navy

Air Force

Marines

Uniforms of the Armed Forces

Cut out these paper figures and dress them in the different uniforms of U.S. military branches (pages 26–29).

Color Key

T-shirt: white

shoes: black

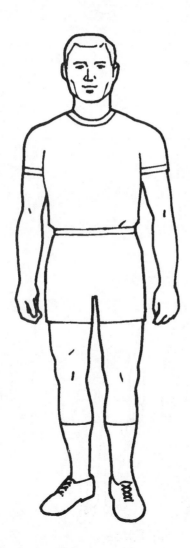

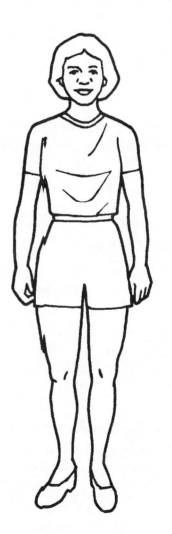

Uniforms of the Armed Forces *(cont.)*
Army

Color Key

pants: green

jacket: green with gold buttons

insignia: gold and black

tie: black

shirt: white

hat: green with gold insignia and black flap

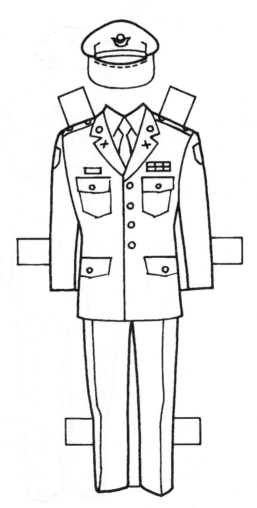

Uniforms of the Armed Forces *(cont.)*
Navy

Color Key

pants: navy blue

skirt: navy blue

jacket: navy blue with gold buttons and gold stripes

shirt: white (men); navy blue with red stripes and white badge (women)

hat: white with navy blue trim

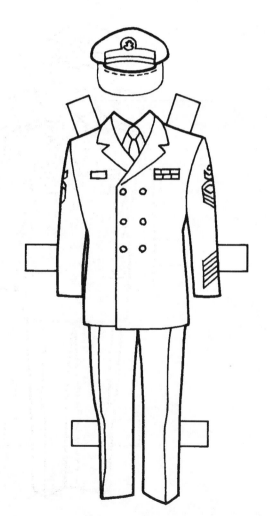

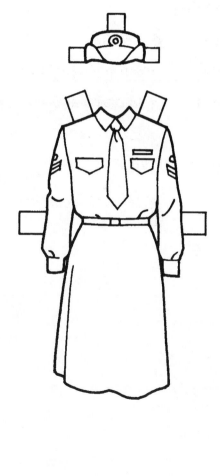

Uniforms of the Armed Forces *(cont.)*

Air Force

Color Key

pants: navy blue

skirt: navy blue

jacket: navy blue; silver insignia, buttons, and
          badges

shirt: white

tie: navy blue

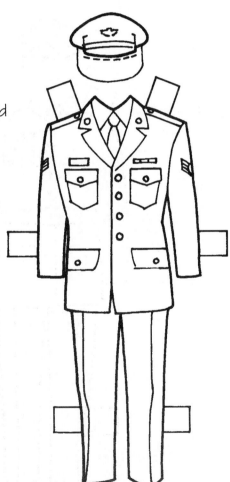

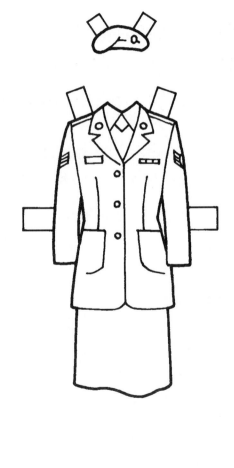

Uniforms of the Armed Forces *(cont.)*

Marines

Color Key

pants: blue

skirt: dark khaki

shirt: navy blue (men); light khaki (women)

hat: white (men); dark khaki (women)

shoes: black

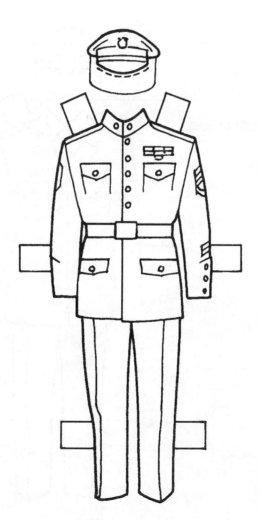

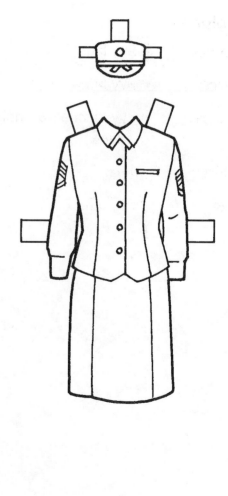

Thanksgiving Day

Thanksgiving Day is a day of gratitude. It is set aside for all people in the United States to join together to give thanks for the good things in their lives. This oldest U.S. holiday tradition began with a feast in October 1621.

In 1619 a courageous group of English men, women, and children seeking religious freedom set sail on the *Mayflower* to journey to a new land. These Pilgrims arrived in Plymouth, Massachusetts, in 1620, ready to begin new lives in the New World.

The first year was very difficult. The winter was harsh, and of the 110 people who sailed from England, fewer than 50 survived. By March their situation had grown desperate. With no food and too weak to begin planting,

they were approached by Samoset, a Native American, who introduced them to Squanto, the man who helped the Pilgrims survive. He taught them how to tap maple trees for sap, where to fish and hunt, and how to plant native crops such as corn, beans, and squash. He showed them how to mound the earth into little hills and to plant the seeds with a fish in each mound for fertilizer.

After the fall harvest, the Pilgrims had much to celebrate. They wanted to thank God for the rich bounty of their harvest and for helping them live through the difficult times. Governor William Bradford proclaimed a feast of thanksgiving. Squanto and other Native Americans joined in the three-day celebration.

Thanksgiving Day *(cont.)*

Squanto showed the Pilgrims how to grow corn, which became a staple, or basic part, of their diet. Often the Pilgrims ate some form of corn at every meal. Pilgrims also found use for a small, sour, red berry they called a craneberry because the plant it grew on resembled the long neck and head of a crane. Native Americans used the juice of these berries to dye wool and to help heal wounds. Cranberries were eaten fresh or ground up and mashed with cornmeal and baked into bread.

In 1789, George Washington made Thanksgiving Day a nationwide event for the people of the original 13 states to rejoice and give thanks for the United States' victory over England in the Revolutionary War. In 1863, President Abraham Lincoln proclaimed the last Thursday in November as National Thanksgiving Day. In 1941 Congress established Thanksgiving Day as the fourth Thursday in November.

Find Out More

. . . in a Book

Sarah Morton's Day by Kate Waters (Scholastic, 1993).

Samuel Eaton's Day by Kate Waters (Simon and Schuster Children's, 1995).

These books feature photographs of real children acting as interpretive guides at Plimoth Plantation in Massachusetts.

Three Young Pilgrims by Cheryl Harness (Bradbury Press, 1992). This touching book tells the story of the Pilgrims through the eyes of the Allerton children.

. . . on the Web

http://craftsforkids.miningco.com/msub13.htm—Find many fun Thanksgiving crafts, coloring sheets, games, poems, and songs.

Pilgrim Hat

What You Need

- grey or brown construction paper
- black construction paper
- scissors
- tape
- glue
- dinner-size paper plate

What To Do

1. Cut out the inside circle of a paper plate. Check to make certain that the opening fits the child's head.

2. Cut a black strip 18" x 2" (46 cm x 5 cm).

3. Cut a grey or brown strip 18" x 6" (46 cm x 15 cm).

4. Glue or tape the black strip to the long edge of the grey/brown strip.

5. Tape the 6" sides together so that the cylinder created fits into the circle cut from the paper plate.

6. Tape the inside of the cylinder to the paper plate.

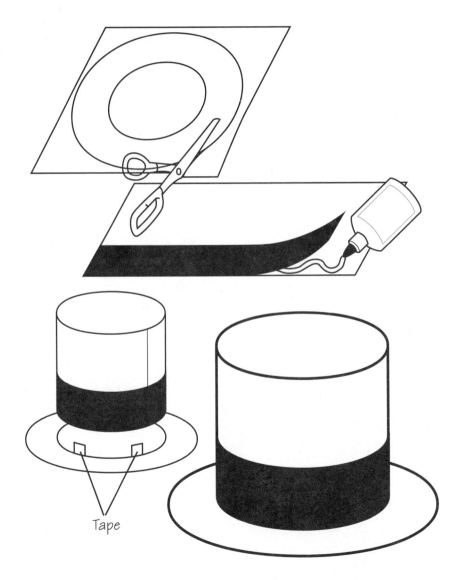

Tape

Pilgrim Bonnet

What You Need

- 2" x 15" (5 cm x 37.54 cm) white poster board
- white tissue paper
- scissors
- glue stick
- stapler
- 36" (91 cm) of white ribbon or yarn

What To Do

1. Glue the tissue paper along the edge of the poster board, gathering in excess length to fit. Allow it to dry.

2. Take the end of the tissue that is not glued to the strip and gently fold it in half. Glue these two edges together. If desired for fit, glue or tape two tucks on the back neck edge.

3. Punch a hole in each end of the front band. Tie half of the ribbon through one hole and half through the other. Tie the two halves under the chin.

Pilgrim Collar

What You Need

- 12" x 18" (30 cm x 46 cm) piece of gray or white paper
- scissors

What To Do

Follow the diagram to create collars.

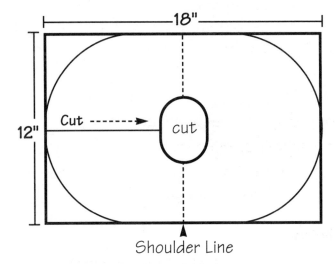

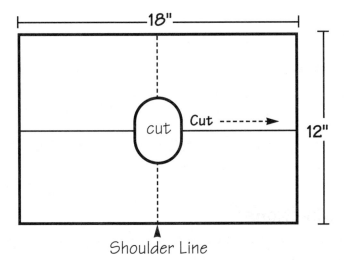

Thanksgiving Recipes

Corn Muffins

Ingredients

- 1 cup (250 mL) flour
- 1 tablespoon (15 mL) baking powder
- $^1/_3$ cup (85 mL) sugar
- $^3/_4$ teaspoon (3.75 mL) salt
- 1 cup (250 mL) cornmeal
- 1 egg
- $^1/_3$ cup (85mL) melted butter
- 1 cup (250 mL) milk

Directions

Preheat the oven to 375° F. Grease the muffin tins or use paper liners. Stir together the flour, baking powder, sugar, and salt. Add the cornmeal. In a separate bowl, beat together the egg, butter, and milk. Add this mixture to the dry ingredients and stir until just wet. Pour the mixture into the muffin cups and bake for 15–20 minutes.

Sweet Popcorn

The Indians brought popped corn to the first Thanksgiving. It became a favorite with the colonists and was eaten like cereal for breakfast or for dinner. Share a treat of popcorn to celebrate like the Pilgrims did!

Ingredients

- plain popcorn (unbuttered, unsalted)
- $^1/_4$ cup butter or margarine
- $^1/_2$ cup brown sugar
- 2 teaspoons light corn syrup

Directions

Pop the popcorn, using your favorite method. Pour the popped corn into a large bowl and set aside. Mix together brown sugar, corn syrup, and butter in a small pan, and heat the mixture until it simmers. Pour the sugar mixture over the popcorn and stir. Let cool before eating.

Thanksgiving Recipes

Cranberry Sauce

Ingredients

- 2 cups (500 mL) boiling water
- 4 cups (1000 mL) cranberries
- 2 cups (500 mL) sugar

Directions

Wash the cranberries. Place them in a saucepan and cover them with the boiling water. When the water begins to boil again, cover the pan and boil for 3–4 minutes. Put the cranberries through a strainer and then back into the saucepan. Add the sugar. Bring the strained cranberries and sugar to a boil. Remove the cranberries from the heat at once. Serve them when cool.

Succotash

Ingredients

- water
- 4 ears of corn
- 10-ounce (275 g) box of frozen lima beans
- salt
- pepper
- 1–2 tablespoons (15–30 mL) butter

Directions

Scrape the corn kernels off the cobs with a knife. Put the kernels and lima beans in a saucepan, and add enough water to cover them. Cook over medium heat about 10–15 minutes or until the vegetables are heated through. Drain off the water. Stir in the butter and season with salt and pepper to taste.

Heroes

Eleanor Roosevelt

Eleanor Roosevelt was born October 11, 1884. She grew up with the strong belief that she had the responsibility to leave the world a better place.

In 1905 she married her distant cousin Franklin Delano Roosevelt. After Roosevelt was elected president of the United States in 1932, First Lady Eleanor continued her humanitarian work. President Harry Truman called her the First Lady of the World. Eleanor Roosevelt was a woman of action, a friend to the poor and oppressed, and a champion of human rights.

Later, she was chosen to serve as a delegate to the United Nations and was elected the chairperson of the United Nation's Commission for Human Rights. Through her efforts, the Universal Declaration of Human Rights was written. She died in 1962, leaving a worldwide legacy of caring.

Find Out More

. . . in a Book

Eleanor by Barbara Cooney (Viking, 1996). This is a wonderful picture book of Mrs. Roosevelt's early years.

A Picture Book of Eleanor Roosevelt by David A. Adler (Holiday House, Inc., 1991).

. . . on the Web

http://myhero.com/hero.asp.hero=eleanorRoosevelt—Read what Eleanor had to say about freedom fighters. You can also participate in the My Hero project.

Helping Hands Wreath

What You Need

- paper plate
- scissors
- pencil
- construction paper
- ribbon
- glue

What To Do

1. Cut the center out of a paper plate, leaving about a 2" (5 cm) rim.

2. Trace your hand several times on different colors of construction paper and cut out the tracings.

3. Glue the paper hands around the rim of the plate, overlapping them.

4. Glue a loop of ribbon for a hanger on the back of the wreath.

Sally Ride

It takes a very special person to be an astronaut. An astronaut must be in excellent health and physical shape. He or she must be a good learner and do well in math and science and be able to solve problems calmly, quickly, and logically. An astronaut needs self-confidence and the strong will to succeed—and he or she must be a team player, able to work well with others to meet a goal. Sally Ride is one of these very special people.

Sally Kristen Ride was born May 26, 1951, in Los Angeles, California. Sally attended Stanford University in California, where she earned a bachelor of arts degree in English and a bachelor of science degree in physics. She went on to earn both a master's degree and doctorate in physics. While working on her doctorate, she read an advertisement by the National Aeronautics and Space Administration (NASA). They were looking for young scientists to become future astronauts.

Sally applied to the program and was selected out of more than 8,000 applicants to be one of the 35 people in the astronaut class of 1978. Dr. Ride was chosen in 1982 to be a mission specialist and flight engineer—and first American woman in space—on the seventh space shuttle flight.

Dr. Sally Ride's success as an astronaut and as a scientist helped broaden opportunities available to other women. Her success is an inspiration to thousands of young people throughout the world to continue to follow their dreams.

Find Out More

. . . on the Web

http://starchild.gsfc.nasa.gov/—Find out about our universe, astronauts, space travel, and more.

Balloon Rocket

What You Need

- long balloon
- string or yarn
- large straw with a short piece cut off
- tape
- measuring tape

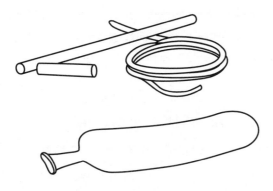

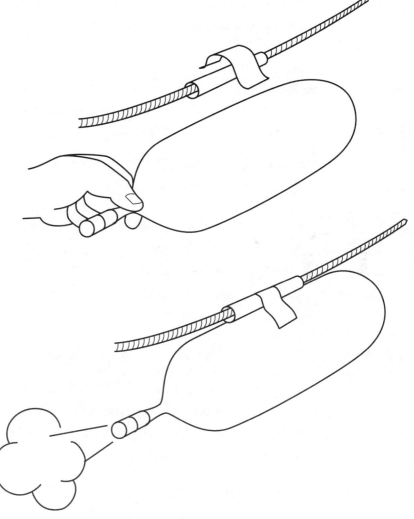

What To Do

1. Place the string or yarn through the longer piece of straw. Attach the string or yarn to each side of the room

2. Blow up the balloon. Do not let the air out. You may wish to use something to clamp the neck of the balloon closed.

3. Tape the longer piece of straw to the balloon, making sure not to let the air out.

4. Place the shorter piece of straw into the neck of the balloon and tape it into place.

5. Stand at one end of the room and let the air out of the balloon. As the air rushes out, the balloon should travel along the string or yarn.

Cesar Chavez

Chavez believed that farm workers needed a strong union to fight for their rights and to improve their conditions. In 1962 he formed the United Farm Workers (UFW), and in 1968 this union was involved in a struggle with the growers over working conditions and the pesticides sprayed on crops. The UFW called a strike, which means union members walked off the job in protest and would not work for the growers until they fixed the problems. The UFW also asked people to show support for farm workers by boycotting, or refusing to buy, California grapes, wine, and lettuce.

Cesar Chavez believed in nonviolence, and he began a hunger strike on February 14, 1968, that caught the attention of news reporters. As the news spread, people from all over the country boycotted the products, and other unions called strikes to show their support for the UFW. The growers were finally forced to sign contracts with the UFW to improve conditions. Chavez continued to champion the rights of farm workers and consumers until his death in 1993.

Cesar Chavez was born in Yuma, Arizona, on March 31, 1927. His family became migrant farm workers, following the harvest to California. The life of a migrant farm worker can be harsh. Housing may be inadequate and food scarce. Children often miss school to work beside their parents.

Find Out More

. . . in a Book

The Tortilla Factory by Gary Paulsen (Harcourt, Brace and Co., 1995). Where do tortillas come from? This book will show you—from farmers to pickers to bakers to the table.

Cesar Chavez (cont.)

Appreciation Salad

Ingredients

- lettuce
- grapes
- sliced strawberries
- sliced bananas
- 8-ounce (225 g) carton vanilla yogurt
- 16-ounce (450 g) carton cottage cheese

Directions

Carefully and thoroughly wash the ingredients. Line a salad plate with large lettuce leaves. Mix the cottage cheese and yogurt together in a bowl. Put a scoop of the cheese-yogurt mixture on top of the lettuce. Spoon the fruit on top of the mixture.

Grape Juice

Ingredients

- red or purple grapes
- water
- sugar

Directions

Wash the grapes and place in a large pot. Add just enough water to cover the grapes. Slowly bring the grapes to a simmer, and let them simmer until they are very soft—about 10 minutes. Drain the juice into another container, then strain it through a coffee filter or several layers of cheesecloth. Add sugar to the juice, about 1 cup per quart. Taste to check sweetness. Heat to a simmer, then skim any foam. Pour the juice into a pitcher or bottle and keep refrigerated.

Harriet Tubman

Harriet Tubman was born in slavery around 1821. Harriet had to work hard from the time she was very young. In 1849, Harriet's master died, and she learned that she and her family were to be sold. Harriet and her brothers decided to escape. They left their home in eastern Maryland in the middle of the night. Her brothers soon turned back, but Harriet headed north alone. With the North Star as her guide, she finally reached Philadelphia.

Harriet was free in Philadelphia, but her friends and family were still in Maryland. She called herself a stranger in a strange land and wrote in her autobiography: "to this solemn resolution I came; I was free, and they should be free also; I would make a home for them in the North, and the Lord helping me, I would bring them all there."

And she did. Over the next 12 years she returned to the South 19 times and smuggled more than 300 people—including her elderly parents—to freedom. Freedom lay in the North. The Fugitive Slave Law of 1850 made it unsafe for runaway slaves to stay anywhere in the United States. It was against the law to help a runaway. People doing so could be fined or jailed. A runaway living in the North could be found by a bounty hunter and forced to return to his or her master.

The fugitives hid by day and traveled by night, often helped along the way by agents on the Underground Railroad. This railroad was neither really underground nor even a real railroad. People who were against slavery hid the fleeing slaves in their homes and helped them get to the next safe place in spite of the dangers to themselves. Harriet never lost a passenger and was never captured herself although there was a $40,000 reward on her head.

Harriet Tubman (cont.)

During the Civil War, Harriet served as a spy, a nurse, a cook, and a scout. She was able to move among the slaves behind Confederate lines and gather useful information for the North. She encouraged slaves to join the Union forces. After the war Harriet Tubman continued to work to improve the lives of former slaves and opened a home for poor and elderly African Americans. She died on March 10, 1913.

Find Out More

. . . in a Book

Aunt Harriet's Underground Railroad in the Sky by Faith Ringgold (Crown Publishing Group, 1995). Take a trip with Cassie as she makes the dangerous journey to freedom.

A Picture Book of Harriet Tubman by David A. Adler (Holiday House, Inc., 1992).

Sweet Clara and the Freedom Quilt by Deborah Hopkinson (Random, 1995). Clara finds a way to help on the Underground Railroad.

. . . on the Web

http://www.ushistory.com/railr.htm—View a music video of "On the Underground Railroad."

Find the North Star

What You Need

- a clear night
- a dark place from which you can see the stars

What To Do

1. Find the group of seven stars that looks like a pan. This is the constellation known as the Big Dipper.

2. The "pointer stars" are the two on the the side of the dipper that is farthest from the handle. Mentally follow a straight line through these two pointer stars to the first very bright star you come to. This is the North Star, and it is always found in the same position.

3. Face the North Star, and you are facing north. Behind you is south. To your right is east, and to your left is west.

Sparkly Star

What You Need

- white pipe cleaner
- widemouthed jar
- water
- thread
- pencil
- measuring cups and spoons
- spoon
- microwave oven
- oven mitt
- borax, 3 tablespoon per cup of water (45 mL borax per 240 mL water)

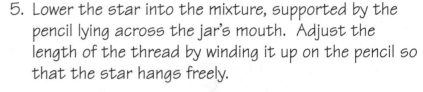

What To Do

1. Bend the pipe cleaner into a star shape.

2. Tie a piece of thread to one of the star's points and tie the other end to a pencil.

3. Put enough water in the jar to submerge the star. Boil the water on high in the microwave.

4. Use oven mitts to carefully remove the jar from the microwave. Stir in the borax until it dissolves.

5. Lower the star into the mixture, supported by the pencil lying across the jar's mouth. Adjust the length of the thread by winding it up on the pencil so that the star hangs freely.

6. Leave the star in the jar overnight. Then take it out and allow it to dry. Discard the borax solution.

7. Cut the pencil off the thread, leaving some thread to use as a hanger attached to the star.

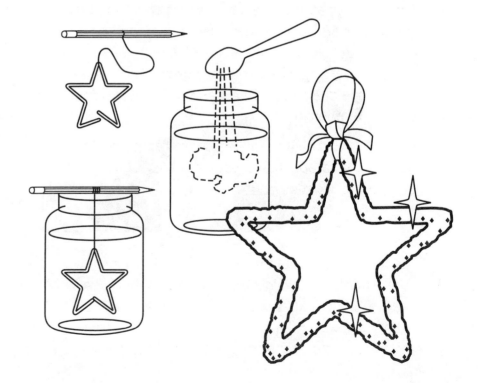

Paul Revere

Paul Revere opposed the Stamp Act, which declared that the American colonists had to buy a British stamp for every piece of printed paper they used. This included newspapers, legal papers, business documents—even playing cards. Paul took part in the Boston Tea Party, helping the Sons of Liberty to dump three shiploads of tea into Boston Harbor to protest the king of Britain's tax on imported English tea.

Paul also was a courier, or messenger. He rode on horseback many times to New York and Philadelphia to carry news of important events. He made his most famous ride on April 18, 1775. A group of American patriots had been gathering gunpowder and cannonballs and storing them in Concord, a little town about 20 miles outside of Boston.

When the British found out about the ammunition, they planned a raid to take it away. The patriots learned of the impending raid and knew they would have to act fast. They devised a system to let the colonists know how the British were going to attack. Someone would hang lanterns in the steeple of North Church—one lantern if the British came by land, two lanterns if they came by sea.

Paul Revere was born January 1, 1735. His father taught young Paul his trade, which was silversmithing. After the elder Revere died, Paul became Boston's leading silversmith. However, Paul Revere is even more famous for his part in the colonies' struggle to free themselves from British rule.

Paul Revere *(cont.)*

The British planned to take a shortcut across the Charles River and travel on to Concord by foot. As soon as their plans were known, two lanterns were hung in the steeple. Paul Revere rowed across the Charles River—his oars wrapped with petticoats to muffle the sound—to Charlestown. There he mounted a waiting horse and rode to Concord to alert the people that the British were coming. Because of the warning, the Minutemen were ready. The "shots heard 'round the world" were fired. The American Revolution had begun.

Find Out More

. . . in a Book

A Picture Book of Paul Revere by David A. Adler (Holiday House, 1995).

Yankee Doodle: A Revolutionary Tail by Gary Chalk (DK Publishing,Inc., 1993). This book starring Revolutionary mice tells the story of American independence with new lyrics to the old favorite, "Yankee Doodle."

. . . on the Web

http://www.paulreverhhouse.org/events/poem.html—This site includes the famous poem "Paul Revere's Ride" by Henry Wadsworth Longfellow.

http://www.ushistory.com/jouett.htm—Find out about Jack Jouett, another American patriot who rode for freedom. Included is a song chronicling the event.

Revere Candlestick

What You Need

- small tomato paste can
- glue (Aleene's Tacky Glue® or hot glue gun)
- small, disposable aluminum pie plate
- scissors
- various shapes of pasta
- silver spray paint

What To Do

1. Use scissors to trim the rim of the pie plate to about 1" (2.54 cm).

2. Bend half of the rim out to form a lip.

3. Glue the can in the center of the pie plate.

4. Glue pasta on the sides of the can and the edges of the pie plate. Allow the glue to dry.

5. Place the candlestick on newspapers in a well-ventilated area and spray it all over with silver spray paint.

6. Put a candle in the holder.

Susan B. Anthony

Susan Brownell Anthony was born February 15, 1820, in Adams, Massachusetts. Her parents were Quakers and raised Susan under the principle that men and women are equal. Beyond her Quaker home, however, the world had a different idea. Susan was allowed to go to school, but even there boys were allowed to do things that girls were not. This made Susan angry, and she did them anyway.

There was so much unfairness and inequality that Susan determined to do something to change the way the world worked. She devoted her life to fighting the injustice of women's inequality. She started in the schools by becoming a teacher. She taught all her students about these inequities.

Later Susan became interested in banning alcohol, feeling that many drinking people became abusive and intolerant under its influence. Frustrated that because she was a woman she was not allowed to publicly speak out about such things, she began her own organization, the Woman's State Temperance Society of New York. During this time, she met Elizabeth Cady Stanton, another woman who shared her beliefs.

That women were not allowed to vote infuriated many women. In 1869, Susan B. Anthony and Elizabeth Cady Stanton formed the National Woman Suffrage Association. Their goal was to get a 19th amendment added to the Constitution of the United States. This amendment would give all women of the United States the right to vote.

Susan felt so strongly about her right to vote that she voted in the 1872 presidential election even though it was illegal for her to do so. Susan actively fought for women's rights for more than 50 years. She gave impassioned speeches, wrote persuasive books and articles, and courageously led women's rights organizations.

Susan B. Anthony *(cont.)*

Susan B. Anthony died in 1906, never seeing one of her fondest dreams realized. It was not until 1920 that the 19th Amendment was added to the Constitution and women were allowed to vote.

Find Out More

. . . in a Book

The Ballot Box Battle by Emily Arnold McCully (Knopf Books, 1996). Elizabeth Cady Stanton is featured in this book.

. . . on the Web

http://www.frintiernet.net/~lhurst/sbahouse/tour0.htm— Tour Susan B. Anthony's house in Rochester, New York, and learn more about this fascinating woman.

http://www.realaudio.com:80/contentp/npr/ne0828.html —Listen to an interview with Judge Lucy Somerville Howorth, a 100-year-old suffragist.

Political Button

What You Need

- metal lid from a juice can
- construction paper scraps
- pencil
- scissors
- glue
- tape
- markers
- 1" (2.54 cm)-wide ribbon
- safety pin

What To Do

1. Trace around the lid onto construction paper and cut out the circle.

2. Write a slogan on the paper circle and glue it to the lid.

3. Cut 4" (10 cm) lengths of ribbon and fold them in half, gluing the loops closed.

4. Glue the loops to the back of the juice lid.

5. Cut two 6" (15 cm) lengths of ribbon and glue them together to form a V. Glue the V to the back of the lid.

6. Glue the safety pin to the back of the lid so you can pin the button on your shirt.

Daniel Boone

Appalachians called Kentucky, where forests were thick with deer, beaver, and wild turkey and where prairies were home to thousands of buffalo.

In 1769, he finally went to Kentucky. He hunted, trapped, and explored. When he returned to North Carolina, he gathered his wife and children, among many others, to move to Kentucky. Daniel led the pioneers through across the Blue Ridge, Appalachian, and Cumberland Mountains. It was a hard and dangerous journey. The pioneers turned back.

In March of 1775, Daniel Boone again made his way west. This time he was prepared to clear a path through the wilderness, across the Cumberland Gap, and into Kentucky. This trail became known as the Wilderness Road. With easier travel, thousands of pioneers flooded into the region, lured by the prospect of good hunting and rich farmland. Daniel Boone had boldly opened the doors to a new land, leading Americans to push ever westward.

Daniel Boone was born in 1734 in a frontier settlement in western Pennsylvania. By the time he was 12, he was a sure shot with a rifle. When Daniel was 17, his family moved to North Carolina. During the French and Indian War, Daniel joined the fight against the French. Then Daniel heard about a wonderful land west of the

Find Out More

. . . on the Web

http://www.truman.edu/academics/fa/faculty/jpaulding/gadkin.html—View an illustrated biography of Daniel Boone's life. Note: There are images of fighting.

Pioneer Pouch

What You Need

- newspapers
- brown paper grocery sack
- gray and brown paint (tempera or acrylic)
- 2 containers for paint
- old toothbrush
- paint brush
- hole punch
- glue
- scissors
- yarn

What To Do

1. Cut the paper sack and lay it in one flat piece.

2. In a container, mix the brown paint with water until it is runny. Brush it on the paper.

3. Pour gray paint into another container. Dip the toothbrush into the paint and use your thumb to flick the paint on the paper. Be sure to move your thumb toward you (not away from you) and point the toothbrush at the paper, or you'll flick the paint all over yourself! Let the paint dry.

4. Cut a pouch, a strap, and a strip for fringe from the paper bag. Fold the pouch into three sections, as shown.

5. Fringe the strip by cutting slits across it. Leave an inch at the top uncut.

6. Punch holes down the sides of the pouch and lace the sides together with yarn.

7. Glue the ends of the strap to the sides of the pouch. Glue the fringe to the bottom.

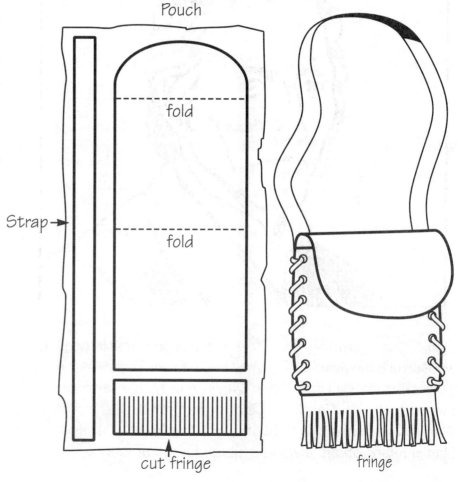

Pouch

Strap →

fold

fold

cut fringe

fringe

John Muir

John Muir, one of America's greatest naturalists and conservationists, was born on April 21, 1838, in Dunbar, Scotland. When he was 11 years old, his family came to the United States. John valued the beauty in the world around him more than anything else. He devoted his life to studying, writing about, and preserving nature.

John Muir traveled the country on foot. In California, he discovered the astonishing beauty of the Yosemite Valley and decided to stay there. A magazine editor encouraged John to write about the beauty of Yosemite Valley and the Sierra Mountains. His writing was instrumental in persuading the public that the preservation of the wilderness was necessary and good.

Muir also proposed that these unique natural areas be kept in trust by a national park system. After President Theodore Roosevelt camped with John Muir in Yosemite, he added his powerful voice to encourage Congress to extend the national forest reserves and to maintain many special areas in their original natural splendor. In 1892, the Sierra Club was formed, and John Muir was its first president. Today the Sierra Club continues its work with the broader mission of protecting the environment and the wilderness.

Find Out More

. . . in a Book

Red Leaf, Yellow Leaf by Lois Ehlert (Harcourt, Brace and Co., 1991). Beautifully vibrant, this book shows the turning of the leaves and gives several tree activities.

. . . on the Web

http://www.myhero.com/hero.asp.hero=johnMuir—This Web site gives more information about John Muir, with links to animations.

http://www.nwf.org/nwf/kids/cool/index.html—This site, designed by the National Wildlife Federation, includes puzzles, quizzes, and information about wetlands, endangered species, water, and public lands.

Nature Journal

What You Need

- 20 sheets of white paper 8½" x 11" (22 cm x 28 cm)
- 2 sheets green construction paper
- strip of brown paper bag 3" x 11" (8 cm x 28 cm)
- raffia or yarn
- hole punch
- glue
- two or three leaves
- wax paper

What To Do

1. Fold a piece of wax paper in half around your leaves. Put some heavy books on top of it and let it sit for about a week, until the leaves are flat and dry.

2. Fold the strip of paper bag in half lengthwise. Punch 10 to 14 holes down it about ½" (1.3 cm) from the fold.

3. Lay the edges of the white and green papers in the fold of the brown strip and mark on them where the holes are.

4. Punch holes in all the papers. Then stack the papers with the white ones in between the green ones.

5. Put the stack of papers inside the brown strip and line up the holes.

6. Use yarn or raffia to lace the book together through the holes. Tie the ends. Glue the leaves to the front cover of your journal.

7. Write one of your own thoughts or a quote by John Muir on the front page of your journal:

"Come to the woods, for here is rest."

"Nature has always something rare to show us."

Clara Barton

Clarissa Harlowe Barton was born in North Oxford, Massachusetts, on Christmas Day in 1821. By the age of 15, she was teaching school. After several years, Clara moved to Washington, D.C., where she took a job as a clerk at the U.S. Patent Office. When the Civil War broke out, wounded Union soldiers poured into the capital.

Clara found busy surgeons dressing soldiers' wounds with cornhusks because they lacked basic supplies. Clara encouraged people to donate medicines and bandages. After nearly a year of lobbying the army, she was allowed to take her own supplies to the battlefields. After the war, Clara helped with the effort to locate or identify unknown Union soldiers reported missing during the Civil War. Her efforts left her physically exhausted, and she went to Europe to rest and recuperate.

While in Switzerland, Clara learned of the International Red Cross, an organization that had been founded in 1864 to provide relief to victims of war. She returned home in 1873 and sought to establish a branch in the United States. In 1881 the American Red Cross was established with Clara Barton as its first president.

Clara served as president for over 20 years, until she was 83. She died in 1912 at the age of 90. Since then, the work of the Red Cross has expanded to include giving aid to victims of natural disasters as well as war. In addition, the Red Cross provides information and training to people in communities across the country.

First Aid Kit

Gather in a box things you might need in case of an injury.

What You Need

- plastic container with lid
- adhesive bandages
- sterile gauze pads
- adhesive tape
- triangular bandages
- sterile roller bandages
- scissors
- needle
- tweezers
- moistened towelettes
- antiseptic
- thermometer
- petroleum jelly
- safety pins
- soap
- sunscreen
- latex gloves

What To Do

1. Keep your first aid kit in a safe and handy place.

2. Keep the telephone number of the Poison Control Center in the box and near your phone.

3. Call your chapter of the American Red Cross and request these pamphlets: "Your Family Disaster Plan" and the "Emergency Preparedness Checklist." Go over these with your family so you are ready in an emergency.

4. Participate in an American Red Cross training course for children. They are First Aid for Children Today (FACT) and Basic Aid Training (BAT).

PARENT: You may wish to include a few nonprescription medications in your first aid kit, such as pain reliever (for adults and for children), antacid, syrup of Ipecac, and activated charcoal (use if advised by Poison Control Center). Remember to keep all medications out of the reach of children.

Sequoyah

12 years working on his syllabary, or system of writing sounds. He discovered that the Cherokee language is made up of clusters of sounds and combinations of vowels and consonants, and he devised 85 symbols that represent all combinations of these sounds.

He demonstrated the system in 1821 to a gathering of tribal leaders, where it was promptly approved. Within a few months, many Cherokee people were able to read and write in their own language. Sequoyah's teaching journeys led him to the mountains of Mexico, where he died in 1843. A statue of Sequoyah, presented by the state of Oklahoma, stands in Statuary Hall in Washington, D.C., and the giant sequoia trees of California were named in his honor.

Find Out More

. . . in a Book

Clever Letters by Laura Allen (Pleasant Company Publications, 1997). This book from the American Girl Library® gives lots of ideas for lettering styles and fun notes to send to your friends.

. . . on the Web

http://www.neosoft.com/powersource/gallery/people/sequoyah.html—The Cherokee alphabet is featured at this site.

Sequoyah was born in the Cherokee village of Tuskegee in Louden County, Tennessee, about 1770. Sequoyah was intrigued by white people's ability to communicate with each other through marks on a piece of paper, called "talking leaves" by some Native Americans. He realized that if his people could communicate in such a way, they could be greater and more powerful.

In 1809, Sequoyah began devising a system of writing the sounds of the Cherokee spoken language. He spent nearly

A New Alphabet

What You Need

- paper
- pencil

What To Do

1. Make a list of the letters in the English alphabet.

2. Invent a new symbol for each letter and write it next to the sound it represents. This is your key.

3. Write your name in the new language. Then write words and sentences.

4. Trade messages with a friend and see whether you can decipher each other's notes.

A   B   C   D   E

F   G   H   I   J

K   L   M   N   O

P   Q   R   S   T

U   V   W   X   Y   Z

Helen Keller

Helen Adams Keller was born on June 27, 1880, in Tuscumbia, Alabama. She was a bright, cheerful, and loving baby, but a serious illness when she was one and a half years old left her suddenly blind and deaf. In this new, frightening, dark, and silent world, she became a wild and temperamental child. Because she could not hear, she could not learn how to speak.

Helen's father wrote to the Perkins Institution for the Blind in Boston. Help arrived in the form of Anne Sullivan, a remarkable teacher. Anne wanted to teach Helen more than just how to behave and take care of herself. She was determined that Helen Keller would learn to communicate.

Anne constantly "finger-spelled" words into Helen's hand, using the manual finger alphabet. At first, Helen did not understand that these motions meant the names of things around her. One morning at the water pump it all came together for her. Anne pumped cold water over Helen's hands while spelling "w-a-t-e-r" into Helen's open hand. Finally, it all made sense! Now Helen wanted to know the name for everything. She had discovered the power of words.

Helen Keller *(cont.)*

Anne took Helen to Boston to the Perkins Institution, where Helen learned to read Braille, an alphabet of raised dots. Helen took lessons from a teacher of the deaf to learn to speak. Amazingly, she also went to college. Anne went with her to finger-spell the professors' words into her hand. In 1904, the seemingly impossible had happened—the young woman who was once entirely unable to communicate had graduated with honors.

Helen spoke and wrote about her life, visiting many nations with her message of hope. On June 1, 1968, Helen Keller died peacefully in her sleep, leaving the world with a changed attitude toward people with disadvantages.

Find Out More:

. . . in a Book

Helen Keller: Courage in the Dark by Johanna Hurwitz (Random House, 1997). This Step into Reading® book tells more about Helen's life and includes the Braille alphabet.

A Picture Book of Helen Keller by David A. Adler (Holiday House, 1992).

. . . on the Web

http://www.afb.org/photos.html—This Web site contains an extensive collection of photographs of Helen Keller at all ages.

Different Alphabets for Hearing and Sight Impaired People

Spartan Alphabet

The "speaker" spells words into the "listener's" hand, using capital letters. Have a friend close his eyes while you write a word on his palm. Remember to use all capital letters. Start with a short word until he gets comfortable with it. Take turns. To say "Yes," make two taps on the person's palm. To say "No" or to erase what you just wrote, make a rub-out motion on the person's palm.

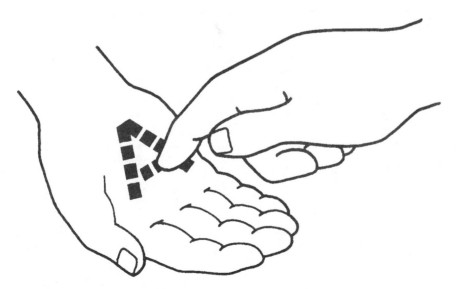

The Manual Alphabet

This manual alphabet is used by some deaf people who can see.

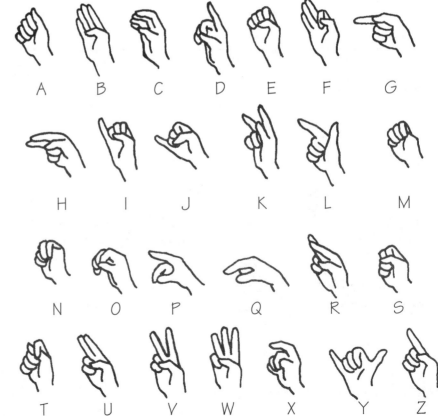

Symbols

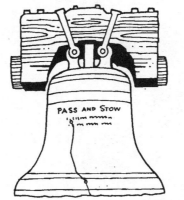

Liberty Bell

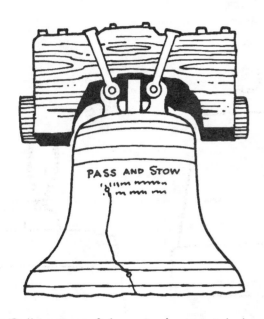

The Liberty Bell is one of America's most beloved symbols of independence and freedom. The bell is proudly diplayed in the Liberty Bell Pavilion in Philadelphia, Pennsylvania. It is made of cast iron, stands nearly 36" (91 cm) high, and weighs about a ton. Its inscription reads: "Proclaiming Liberty throughout all the Land unto all the Inhabitants thereof."

The bell was first rung when it arrived in America in 1752. The first time the clapper hit the bell's side, the bell cracked. Workers in Philadelphia recast it twice to fix it. On July 8, 1776, the bell rang out to announce the first reading of the Declaration of Independence to the people of Philadelphia. It rang for the reading of the Proclamation of Peace with England and the adoption of the Constitution of the United States. In 1835, the bell cracked and was repaired for the third time.

While ringing for George Washington's birthday in 1846, the Liberty Bell cracked yet again. This time it could not be repaired, and it was taken down from the belfry. Even though it can no longer ring out its message of freedom, the Liberty Bell remains a symbol of America's founding principles of independence and democracy.

Find Out More

. . . on the Web

http://nw3.nai.net/~spyder/home.htm—Hear the "Liberty Bell March" by John Phillip Sousa and find out where in your state you can visit an exact replica of the Liberty Bell.

Clay Liberty Bell

What You Need

- small clay flower pot
- 24" (61 cm) of twine
- wooden beads
- gray acrylic paint
- permanent black marker

What To Do

1. Paint the outside of the pot gray and let it dry thoroughly.

2. Use the black marker to draw a jagged "crack" on the bell. Write "Proclaiming Liberty" around the rim.

3. Fold the piece of twine in half and tie a knot about five inches from the fold, forming a loop for a hanger.

4. Thread a bead onto the loop and then stick the loop inside the pot and up through the hole in the bottom. The bead will keep the twine from pulling completely out of the hole.

5. Thread another bead onto the loop and pull it until it is snug to the pot. Secure that bead with a knot in the loop.

6. Make a clapper by threading beads onto the two loose ends of the twine. Be sure to tie the beads high enough so they will hit the inside of the pot. Cut off excess twine.

7. Hang your bell.

The Bald Eagle

The eagle has long been a symbol of strength and power. Countries and even empires have chosen the eagle as their symbol. So when it came time to choose a national bird for America, many wanted it to be the eagle. But not everyone agreed.

Benjamin Franklin proposed that the turkey be the national bird because it was a true native of their new country. However, in 1782 the Congress chose the bald eagle, a bird also unique to North America but perhaps a more fitting symbol for a strong and brave new nation.

The bald eagle is not really bald. The head and tail feathers of an adult bird are white. To the early English people, "bald" meant "white" or "white-streaked," not "hairless." The bald eagle still serves as a symbol of the size and strength of our nation. On our dollar bill, the bald eagle holds an olive branch, a symbol of peace, in its right talon. In its left talon, the eagle holds arrows, a symbol of strength.

Find Out More

. . . on the Web

http:www.eagles.org/all.html—This Web site, dedicated to the preservation and protection of the American bald eagle, contains lots of great pictures and information. Listen to the "Save the Eagle®" song.

Eagle Mask

What You Need

- paper plate
- scissors
- transparent tape
- hole punch
- large rubber band
- yellow marker or crayon
- glue
- small white craft feathers

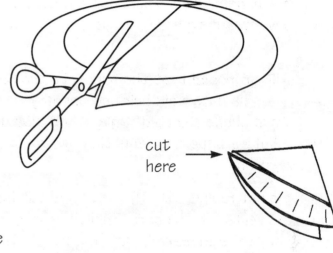

cut here

What To Do

1. Cut the paper plate in half. Half will be the mask face, and the other half will be the beak.

2. Fold one of the paper plate pieces in half and cut the corner off to make a beak. Color the beak yellow.

3. On the flat side of the face plate, punch a hole on both sides.

4. Hold the face plate to your face and carefully mark where your eyes are. Cut two eyeholes.

5. Tape the beak onto the face plate.

6. Glue feathers onto the face plate.

7. Cut the rubber band open and tie each end to one of the holes in the plate. Put on your eagle mask.

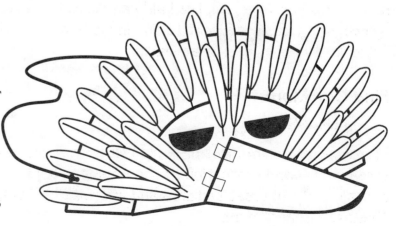

United States Flag

One of our most beloved national symbols is the American flag. It has changed many times over the years. The first American flag had 13 stars and 13 stripes to symbolize the original 13 colonies.

The colors chosen for the flag were important, too. The stripes alternated red and white, and the five-pointed stars lay on a blue background. Red symbolized valor or bravery. White stood for purity and goodness, and blue represented justice and fairness.

The plan was to add a stripe and a star each time a new state joined the union. It didn't take long for people to realize that if this plan were followed, the flag would quickly become much too large. Congress voted in 1818 to retain the 13 stripes in recognition of the original states and to add a star for every new state therafter. Our flag now has 50 stars, and red, white, and blue are colors associated with America.

Here are some guidelines for honoring the flag:

1. Display the flag only between dawn and dusk.

2. Make sure the stars are on upper left side.

3. Carfully fold the flag and put it away when it's not being displayed.

4. Do not let the flag touch the ground.

5. Burn worn-out flags to destroy them.

Find Out More

. . . on the Web

http://www.legion.org/flagtoc.htm—This site shows how to properly fold the flag and describes the symbolism involved in the flag-folding ceremony.

http://www.ushistory.org/betsy/flagstar.html—Find out how to cut a five-pointed star with just one snip of your scissors.

Folding the Flag

Here is how to correctly fold an American flag.

1.

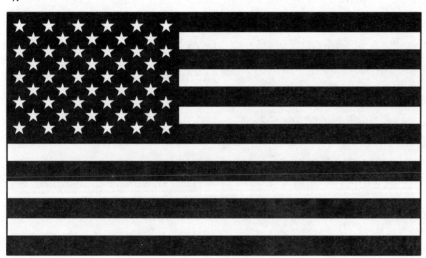

2.

3.

4.

5.

6.

"The Star-Spangled Banner"

President James Madison sent Francis Scott Key, a lawyer and a friend of Dr. Beanes, to Baltimore to get the British to release Dr. Beanes. He was successful, but the two Americans were not allowed to return to Baltimore. The British were about to attack Fort McHenry.

From the British ship, Key and Beanes watched the battle. It began at dawn on September 13 and continued through the night. The next morning, Francis Scott Key was so happy to see the American flag still flying that he wrote a poem, "The Defense of Fort McHenry," about how he felt. That poem was later set to music and called "The Star-Spangled Banner." Congress officially made "The Star-Spangled Banner" our national anthem in 1931.

Find Out More

. . . in a Book

The Star-Spangled Banner by Peter Spier (Bantam Doubleday Dell Books for Young Readers, 1992). This book contains the words and music for four verses of the song, as well as an illustrated evolution of the American flag from the time of the Revolution.

In 1812 America went to war against England again. The English wanted America to stop trading with the French, and they were taking sailors from American ships. The British attacked the new capital, Washington, D.C., and burned the president's house and other buildings in 1814. When they went back to their ships, they took Dr. William Beanes as a prisoner because Dr. Beanes had arrested British soldiers.

Star-Spangled Windsock

What You Need

- red and white crepe paper streamers
- blue construction paper, 9" x 18" (23 cm x 46 cm)
- glue
- stapler
- scissors
- tape
- white chalk or silver glitter
- yarn or string

What To Do

1. Use white chalk or glue silver glitter to make stars on one side of the blue paper.

2. Form the construction paper into a short cylinder with the stars on the outside. Glue and staple it closed.

3. Form a hanger by cutting three 12" (30 cm) lengths of string or yarn. Space them equally around the top of the cylinder and tape them. Knot the strings together.

4. Glue red and white streamers to the other end, and hang your windsock outdoors.

The Pledge of Allegiance

What does it mean to "pledge allegiance" to something or someone? It means you promise to be true and faithful, and when we pledge allegiance to the flag of the United States, we promise to support and be faithful to our country.

Francis Bellamy of Boston, Massachusetts, wrote the Pledge of Allegiance in 1892. Like the flag itself, the pledge has changed throughout the years. In 1942, Congress made the pledge an official vow of loyalty to the United States. In 1954, the words "under God" were added.

Here are the correct words to our Pledge of Allegiance.

"I pledge allegiance to the flag of the United States of America and to the republic for which it stands, one nation under God, indivisible, with liberty and justice for all."

Pledge of Allegiance Sampler

What You Need

- white cotton fabric
- blue and red cotton fabric pieces
- 4 red buttons
- star-shaped buttons
- fine-point, permanent black marker

- needle
- scissors
- thread
- glue
- 8" (20 cm) dowel
- 12" (30 cm) ribbon or yarn

What To Do

1. Cut out a square from white material.

2. Make a sleeve for the dowel by folding a short side over 1" (2.54 cm) and stitching close to the cut edge.

3. Cut a square from the blue and stripes from the red material and arrange in a flag design in the middle of the white square. Glue or sew the pieces in place.

4. Sew star buttons on the blue and a red button in each corner of the sampler. Do not stitch a button on the dowel sleeve.

5. Use the marker to write the Pledge of Allegiance on the sampler.

6. Slip the dowel through the sleeve and tie each end with yarn or ribbon to form a hanger.

Note: Practice writing with the marker on a scrap of fabric before writing on your sampler.

I Pledge

Uncle Sam

Who is that tall, bearded man wearing striped pants, a long tailcoat, and a tall hat covered with stars and stripes? It's Uncle Sam. There are several stories about how this figure become a symbol of the United States, but this is the one Congress officially recognized in 1961.

Samuel Wilson was born in Arlington, Massachusetts, in 1766. Later he moved to Troy, New York, and started a meatpacking business. During the War of 1812, Sam Wilson supplied meat to the United States Army in barrels marked "U.S." When asked what the initials stood for, one of Wilson's workers said they stood for the meatpacker, Uncle Sam Wilson. The story gained popularity when it was printed in a New York City newspaper. Soon many things labeled U.S. were being called Uncle Sam's.

Illustrators began to draw Uncle Sam as a symbol of the United States, using the same colors and stars-and-stripes designs as the American flag. In 1869 a famous cartoonist named Thomas Nast gave Uncle Sam a beard. During World War I, artist James Flagg used Uncle Sam on an army recruiting poster. On the poster, Uncle Sam points a finger at the person looking at him and says, "I Want You!"

Uncle Sam Hat

What You Need

- large paper plate
- large oatmeal container
- blue strip of construction paper, 2½" x 18" (6.3 cm x 46cm)
- red and white construction paper
- two 12" (30 cm) lengths of red, white, or blue yarn
- glue
- tape

What To Do

1. Glue or tape white construction paper around the container.

2. Glue or tape on red construction paper stripes vertically to the white paper.

3. Cover the bottom of the container with a red paper circle. Leave the top uncovered.

4. To make the hat's brim, trace the container's opening on the paper plate. Add four tabs to the inside of the circle. Cut out the brim, being careful not to cut off the tabs.

5. Attach the brim to the container's opening, taping the tabs to the inside of the container.

6. Decorate the blue strip with white stars and glue it around the container just above the brim.

7. Poke two holes on opposite sides of the brim. Tape or tie the ends of the yarn through the holes.

8. Put on your hat and tie the yarn under your chin.

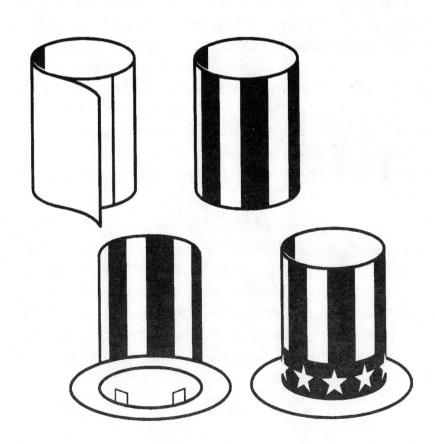

Statue of Liberty

The people of France had watched and admired the struggle for democracy and freedom of 13 small colonies against the great British empire. France decided to give the United States a gift that would be a tribute to this liberty, as well as a symbol of the friendship between their two countries.

Frederic Auguste Bartholdi, a sculptor, sailed to the United States to find support and a location for France's gift. He and President Ulysses Grant agreed that France would build the statue, and the United States would build the base and pedestal. Funds for the huge statue were raised by the French people.

Bartholdi designed the figure of a robed woman with her right arm holding a flaming torch high above her head. Construction on "Lady Liberty" began in a Paris workshop in 1875. By July 4, 1876, Bartholdi had completed only the right hand and the torch, which he sent to the United States for their centennial celebration of the signing of the Declaration of Independence.

The completed statue was officially presented to representatives of the United States in Paris, France, on July 4, 1884. It was then carefully taken apart and shipped across the ocean to America. The statue arrived in 1885, and the pedestal was completed in April of 1886.

Statue of Liberty (cont.)

The statue, called Liberty Enlightening the World, is a national monument and a symbol of many things. The lady herself represents freedom and independence. The tablet in her left hand represents the Declaration of Independence. She holds the Torch of Freedom high in her right hand. A broken chain near her feet represents the victory of liberty over tyranny. The spikes on her crown reach to the seven seas and the seven continents and stand for seven liberties—civil, moral, national, natural, personal, political, and religious.

Over the years, Liberty Enlightening the World has become known as the Statue of Liberty. American poet Emma Lazarus wrote the poem that was placed on the pedestal in 1903. The words gave, and continue to give, a message of hope to all who wish to settle in our land. The poem ends with these famous lines:

> "Give me your tired, your poor,
> Your huddled masses yearning to breathe free,
> The wretched refuse of your teeming shore.
> Send these, the homeless, tempest-tost to me,
> I lift my lamp beside the golden door!"

Find Out More

. . . on the Web

http://www.sccorp.com/cam/—This Web site includes a live shot of the Statue of Liberty.

http://www.libertystatepark.com/statueof.htm—Ever wonder about the size of Lady Liberty's fingernail or the length of her nose? This site will give you these statistics and more.

Liberty Crown and Torch

The Statue of Liberty is made of copper, which eventually turns green when exposed to air and the elements.

What You Need

- 7 pieces of green copy paper
- green construction paper
- yellow tissue paper
- stapler, tape, or glue
- scissors

What To Do

Crown

1. From the construction paper, cut a strip 2½" (6.3 cm) wide and long enough to fit around your head. You may need to tape two pieces together to make it long enough. Staple or tape the band closed.

2. Roll the copy paper into cones for the crown's spikes. Tape each cone closed, keeping the pointed end tightly wrapped. Ask a helper to tape the cones together while you hold them so they don't unroll.

3. When all seven cones have been rolled, use scissors to cut the open ends so they are level.

4. Make tabs in the cones by cutting ½" (1.3 cm) slits around the open parts.

5. Press each cone onto the headband and tape the tabs to the headband.

Torch

Roll green construction paper into a cone. Tape or glue it closed. Stuff yellow tissue paper into the cone to look like a flame.

Monuments and Memorials

Washington Monument

George Washington, known as the Father of Our Country, was born February 22, 1732, in Virginia. He lived on an estate called Mount Vernon. According to legend, young George Washington chopped down one of his father's cherry trees. When confronted, he said, "I cannot tell a lie. I did cut it with my hatchet." While we now know this story is probably not true, it shows the nature of Washington's character and the importance he placed on telling the truth.

When George was 21 he joined the army and fought in the French and Indian War. He was a good leader and a brave soldier. After the war he went home to Mount Vernon to become a farmer. He met and married a young widow named Martha.

War broke out between Great Britain and the new American colonies. The Continental Army needed a capable leader, and Congress decided that George Washington was that person. Washington and his men faced a harsh and bitterly cold winter (1777–1778) at Valley Forge, Pennsylvania. Many died.

After the war, some people wanted George Washington to be king. But many colonists, including Washington, didn't want their new nation to be ruled by a king. Instead, in 1789, Washington was elected the first President of the United States. He was elected to a second term and refused to run for a third.

Washington Monument *(cont.)*

George Washington died on December 14, 1799. One of his officers, Henry Lee, said that Washington was "First in war, first in peace, and first in the hearts of his countrymen."

The capital of the United States was moved from New York City to the shores of the Potomac and named in George Washington's honor. The monument built to honor him was completed in 1884. The obelisk rises 555 feet, 5 1/8 inches. The inside of it is hollow, with many carved memorial stones set in its inner walls. An interior elevator carries people to the top of the Washington Monument, where they are treated to a spectacular view of the Washington, D.C., area.

Find Out More

. . . in a Book

A Picture Book of George Washington by David A. Adler (Holiday House, 1990).

George Washington: A Picture Book Biography by James Cross Giblin (Scholastic, Inc., 1992). Beautiful illustrations accompany this biography of our first president.

. . . on the Web

http://quiz.mountvernon.org/education/index.html—How much do you know about George Washington? Test yourself at this Web site with an online quiz. Also view a sample of 12-year-old George's handwriting and tour the grounds of Mount Vernon.

http://www.nps.gov/htdocs2/wamo/monument/10tour.htm #Washington National Monument Society—Take a Quicktime virtual tour of the Washington National Monument with National Park Service Ranger Dave.

Cherry Cheese Tarts

What You Need

- 1⅓ cup (85 mL) graham cracker crumbs
- ½ cup (125 mL) sugar
- ¼ cup (63 mL) melted butter or margarine
- 8-ounce (225 g) package of cream cheese, softened
- 1 egg
- 1 teaspoon (5 mL) vanilla
- 1 can cherry pie filling
- muffin pan
- foil cupcake liners
- bowl
- spoon
- mixer
- oven mitt

What To Do

1. Preheat the oven to 350° F. Line the muffin tin with cupcake liners.

2. Mix together the graham cracker crumbs, ¼ cup (63 mL) of sugar, and the melted butter. Place a spoonful of the mixture in each muffin cup and press down to form a crust. Bake for eight minutes and then remove from the oven.

3. While the crusts are baking, mix together the cream cheese, ¼ cup (63 mL) of sugar, the egg, and the vanilla. Beat until the mixture is smooth.

4. Fill each cupcake liner almost to the top with the cheese mixture. Return the muffin tin to the oven and bake the tarts for 10 to 12 minutes.

5. Remove the tarts from the oven and carefully spoon a few cherries on top of each tart.

6. Let the tarts cool and then remove them from the muffin tin. Refrigerate the tarts before serving.

Cherry Tree Art

What You Need

- brown construction paper
- white construction paper
- green tissue
- pencil
- glue
- popped popcorn
- dry red tempera paint
- lunch sack

What To Do

1. Place a handful of popcorn in the lunch sack and add two spoonfuls of dry red tempera. Shake the bag to coat the popcorn.

2. Tear a trunk shape from the brown construction paper and glue it to the white paper.

3. Tear small squares from the green tissue, wrap each piece around the end of the pencil, and glue the pieces onto the tree for leaves.

4. Glue on the red popcorn for cherries.

Note: You may also want to draw in George and his hatchet.

George Washington Activities

Handwriting

George Washington practiced his handwriting by copying from the Rules of Civility and Decent Behavior in Company and Conversation. Three of these rules have been rewritten in more modern terms. Write two rules of your own. Copy them onto "antique" paper (page 87) to practice your own handwriting.

1. Listen closely when someone speaks to you.

2. Think before you speak.

3. Keep your promises.

4.

5.

Washington Minute

What You Need

- index cards
- markers
- timer
- pencil and paper

What To Do

1. Print each letter of George Washington's name on an index card. Use colored markers to decorate the edges of the cards with stars or cherries.

2. Get a partner to play with you and write the words you make.

3. Set the timer for one minute. See how many different words you can form with the cards.

4. Take turns and see who can make the most words in a minute.

Antique Paper

What You Need

- white construction paper
- permanent marker
- coffee or cola
- bowl
- layers of newspaper
- brown tempera paint
- paintbrush
- paint cup or pan

What To Do

1. Tear around the edges of the paper and then write your list of rules (page 86) with the permanent marker.

2. Crumple the paper into a ball and dip it in a bowl of coffee or cola. The longer you leave your paper in the liquid the darker it will be, but don't leave it so long that the paper disintegrates.

3. Spread the paper to dry on layers of newspaper.

4. When the paper is dry, mix brown tempera paint with water in a paint cup or pan to make a thin, watery paint. Lightly brush the edges of the paper with the paint.

Lincoln Memorial

Abraham Lincoln was born on February 12, 1809, in a little log cabin in the backwoods of Kentucky. Lincoln once said that he went to school by "the littles"—a little now and a little then. He loved to read and eagerly read everything he could get his hands on.

When Abraham Lincoln was 21, his family moved to Illinois. He helped his parents build their new house, plow and plant their fields, and build more rail fences. When he was 22, he left his family to be on his own. In 1836 Lincoln took a test to become a lawyer. He moved to Springfield, the new capital of Illinois, and practiced law. In 1842 he married Mary Todd, and four years later he was elected to Congress.

In 1858 Abraham Lincoln was the Republican candidate for the Senate. Though not an abolitionist, he was against slavery, a practice he had seen years before while visiting New Orleans. Lincoln ran against Stephen Douglass, and though he did not win, their debates made him famous. He was devoted to the cause of personal freedom for all people. Abraham Lincoln was elected the sixteenth president of the United States in 1860.

Lincoln Memorial (cont.)

In 1861, the southern states withdrew from the United States and formed the Confederate States of America. The South depended on slaves for their economy, and the North did not believe in slavery. The Civil War broke out, and Lincoln supported keeping the Union intact. On January 1, 1863, he signed the Emancipation Proclamation, freeing all the slaves. Later that year he gave one of his most famous speeches at Gettysburg, Pennsylvania, declaring that government "of the people, by the people, for the people, shall not perish from the earth."

The war ended just as Lincoln was beginning his second term as President. Within days of his inauguration, while he was attending a play at Ford's Theater, Abraham Lincoln was shot and killed.

The Lincoln Memorial is a white marble building with a magnificent marble statue of Lincoln sitting in a chair. Also inside it are tablets with the Gettysburg Address and Lincoln's Second Inaugural Address written on them.

Find Out More

. . . in a Book

Pink and Say by Patricia Polacco (Putnam Publishing Group, 1994). Two boys caught up in the Civil War draw strength from one another and from the hand that touched Abe Lincoln.

Young Abe Lincoln by Cheryl Harness (Simon and Schuster Children's, 1996). This book chronicles the life of young Abe—from frontier boy to the White House.

. . . on the Web

http://www.nh.ultranet.com/~wendyh/lincoln/lincoln.htm.—This site features a biography with illustrations by first-graders and information on publishing writings or drawings of Lincoln in The Lincoln Gallery.

http://www.siec.k12.in.us/~west/lincoln/home.htm—View an animation that shows how the continental USA developed, take an online quiz, or go on an Abe Lincoln treasure hunt and find out how to get in the Abraham Lincoln Treasure Hunt Hall of Fame.

Log Cabin

What You Need

- glue
- pencils
- scissors
- plain brown grocery bags
- brown construction paper

What To Do

1. Cut grocery bags into 5" x 2½" (13 cm x 6.3 cm) strips. Make 20 to 60 strips, depending on how large you want your cabin to be.

2. Form a log by rolling a strip around a pencil and gluing it together. Remove the log from the pencil and let it dry. Make all the strips into logs.

3. Make the walls of the cabin by gluing four to eight logs in a stack for each side of the cabin.

4. Make a roof by cutting a rectangular piece of brown construction paper to fit over the top of the cabin. Glue it into place.

5. Cut and glue more logs onto the roof of the cabin.

6. Cut out a door and a window or make them from colored paper and glue them onto the log cabin.

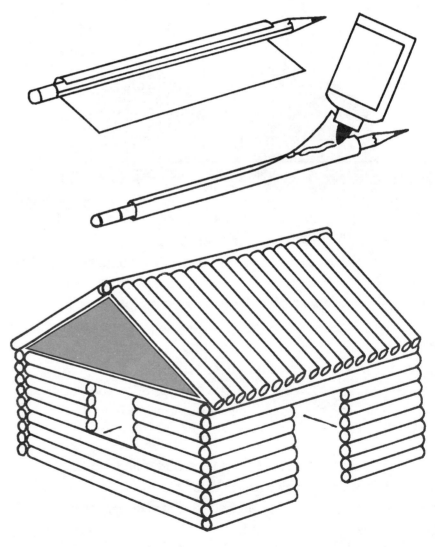

Lincoln Top Hat Bank

What You Need

- empty soup can
- black poster board
- black construction paper
- scissors
- tape
- glue

What To Do

1. Place the soup can on poster board and trace around the can. This will become the top of the hat bank.

2. Cut out the circle and cut a slit in the middle of it so a penny can slip through.

3. Tape this circle to the open end of the can.

4. Again trace the can onto poster board. Cut about 2" (5 cm) around this circle to create the bank's bottom and hat brim.

5. Glue this circle to the bottom of the can.

6. Cut construction paper to fit around the can and glue it into place.

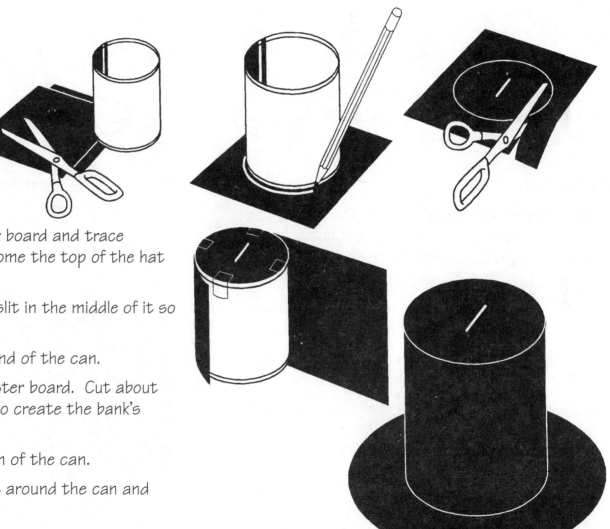

91

Jefferson Memorial

Thomas Jefferson was born on April 13, 1743, in Virginia. When Jefferson was 14, his father died, leaving him more than 2,000 acres of land, his desk, a bookcase, and a library of about 40 books. Thomas Jefferson loved to read and learn. Those books were the start of Jefferson's own personal library, which later grew into the thousands. Jefferson designed and built his own house on a small mountain in Virginia. He called his home Monticello, which means "little mountain."

Thomas Jefferson has been called the "Pen of the American Revolution." He was on the committee that drafted the Declaration of Independence in 1776. Jefferson's words remain as powerful today:

"We hold these truths to be self-evident, that all men are created equal, that they are endowed by their Creator with certain unalienable Rights, that among these are Life, Liberty, and the pursuit of Happiness."

During the Revolutionary War, Jefferson served two terms as governor of Virginia. He served as vice president under John Adams, and in 1801 he became the third president of the United States.

Jefferson Memorial *(cont.)*

Jefferson said "the best government is the least government." He believed in the rights of individual states over the authority of the federal government. In 1803, he bought the Louisiana Purchase from France and almost doubled the size of our young country. He commissioned the Lewis and Clark Expedition (1804–1806) to explore this vast new territory. Jefferson cut taxes and stopped slaves from being brought into the United States.

After two terms as president, Thomas Jefferson returned to Monticello. On July 4, 1826, exactly 50 years after the signing of the Declaration of Independence, Thomas Jefferson died.

The Thomas Jefferson Memorial was dedicated on April 13, 1943, the 200th anniversary of his birth. A white marble dome tops this beautiful circular building that has an outside portico, or porch, supported by 12 columns. Inside is a bronze statue of Jefferson, as well as panels engraved with quotations from his writings.

Find Out More

. . . in a Book

A Picture Book of Thomas Jefferson by David A. Adler (Holiday House, 1990).

Lewis and Clark: Explorers of the Far West by Steven Kroll (Holiday House, 1994). This book beautifully chronicles the journey and adventures of the Corps of Discovery.

. . . on the Web

http://www.monticello.org/index.html—Spend a day with Thomas Jefferson, who rose with the sun and made it a point to read for at least a half an hour before he went to bed. This fascinating site includes a recipe for Monticello Muffins and instructions for the proper way to eat them according to Jefferson's grandson Benjamin Franklin Randolph.

Quill Pen

What You Need

- wing feather from a goose, turkey, seagull, or crow
- sharp knife
- adult help

What To Do

1. With the knife, make an angled cut on the underside of the feather tip.

2. Cut the tip square.

3. Slit the tip just a little.

4. Press the tip open with a pencil.

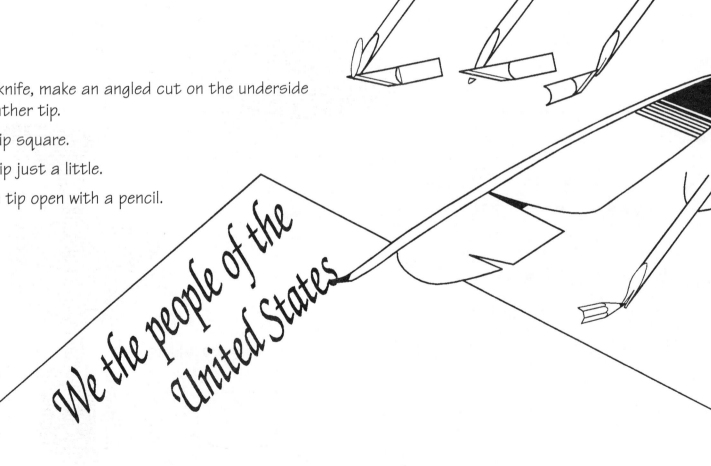

Berry Ink

What You Need

- ½ cup (125 mL) blueberries or strawberries
- ½ teaspoon (2.5 mL) salt
- ½ teaspoon (2.5 mL) vinegar
- measuring cup and spoons
- strainer
- 2 bowls
- wooden spoon
- small jar with tight-fitting lid

What To Do

1. Place the berries in a bowl and use the wooden spoon to crush them, collecting the juice in the bowl.

2. Strain the juice into the second bowl, using the strainer. Throw away the pulp.

3. Stir the salt and vinegar into the juice.

4. Pour the ink into the jar and cover tightly. Store unused ink in the refrigerator.

Nut Ink

What You Need

- 8 whole walnut shells
- nutcracker
- 1 cup (250 mL) water
- ½ teaspoon (2.5 mL) vinegar
- ½ teaspoon (2.5 mL) salt
- measuring cup and spoons
- strainer
- saucepan
- hammer
- piece of cloth
- small jar with tight-fitting lid

What To Do

1. Shell the nuts and set the nutmeat aside.

2. Wrap the shells in cloth and crush them with a hammer. Do this on a hard surface.

3. Place the crushed shells in the saucepan with the water and bring it to a boil. Turn down the heat and simmer on low for 30 minutes.

4. Remove the mixture from the heat and allow to cool to room temperature.

5. Pour the ink through the strainer into the jar, stir in the vinegar and salt, and cover the jar tightly. Store unused ink in the refrigerator.

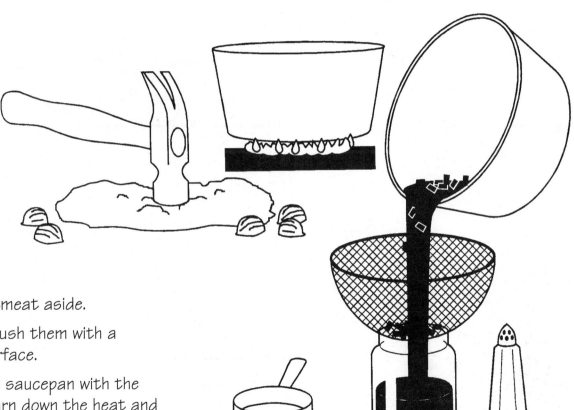

The Capitol

gave land on the Potomac River for the new city, and it was called the District of Columbia.

During the War of 1812, the British stormed Washington, D.C., and burned the Capitol, the President's House, and other public buildings. During the rebuilding of the Capitol, the wing for the members of the Senate and the wing for the members of the House of Representatives were connected by a building covered by a low dome. As the nation grew, the building became so crowded that Congress voted to enlarge the wings and make a higher, cast-iron dome over the connected buildings. On December 2, 1863, in the midst of the Civil War, the Capitol building was finished and topped with the bronze Statue of Freedom.

Inside the Capitol are hundreds of rooms, many of which contain historical collections, famous paintings, and valuable sculptures. The circular space under the dome is called the Rotunda. Covering its ceiling is a huge fresco, or painting, that glorifies George Washington.

When George Washington was president, the capital was in several different cities, including Philadelphia, Boston, and New York. In 1790, Congress appointed a committee to choose a permanent location for the country's capital. They decided that a new city should be built and that it should not be part of any state. Maryland and Virginia

Find Out More

. . . on the Web

http://www2.cr.nps.gov/pad/adventure/landmarks/capital.htm—This site contains a line drawing of the U.S. Capitol building to print out and color.

Make a Fresco

What You Need

- foam meat or bakery tray
- plaster of Paris
- watercolor paints
- paintbrushes

What To Do

1. Mix the plaster of Paris according to the package directions. Make enough to fill your tray.

2. Pour the plaster into the tray.

3. Begin painting right away before the plaster dries. You may wish to paint a nature or patriotic scene.

4. Allow the paint and plaster to dry completely and then remove the fresco from the tray.

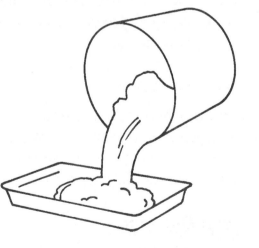

The Tomb of the Unknown Soldier

Throughout history, people in the armed forces of the United States have willingly fought and died for our country and its principles. When a member of the armed forces dies, he or she is given a military funeral with honors. The Tomb of the Unknown Soldier, or Tomb of the Unknowns, honors those soldiers who gave their lives but whose identities were not known.

The tomb is a white marble sarcophagus and is in Arlington National Cemetery, on a hill overlooking Washington, D.C. It has figures representing Peace, Victory, and Valor. Peace holds a palm branch to reward the courageous sacrifice the soldier made for America.

On the back of the tomb is this inscription: "Here rests in honored glory an American soldier known but to God."

The tomb is guarded day and night by members of the elite 3rd U.S. Infantry, also known as The Old Guard. A strict ritual is followed. The sentinel takes 21 steps, turns and faces east for 21 seconds, turns and faces north for 21 seconds and then takes 21 steps back and repeats the process. He must take 90 steps per minute. The number of steps is a symbol of America's highest military honor, the 21-gun salute. After each turn, the guard places his weapon on the shoulder that is farthest from the Tomb to show that he stands between the Tomb and any threat.

Walk the Walk

Get a stopwatch or a watch with a second hand. Go to an open area. Start the stopwatch when you take your first step. Count your steps but don't watch the clock. Can you take 90 steps per minute?

Find Out More

. . . on the Web

http://home.att.net/~Michael.Patterson—This site contains excellent photographs and an extensive list of related links.

White House

The most famous house in America is at 1600 Pennsylvania Avenue in Washington, D.C. It is the White House, the home of the president of the United States, and the oldest government building in Washington. George Washington was to be its first resident, but construction took eight years. The first president to live there was John Adams, our second president.

On New Year's Day in 1801, the Adamses held the first formal reception in an upstairs sitting room. Three months later, Thomas Jefferson was inaugurated as the third president, and he moved in. Jefferson changed the name of the house from the Presidential Palace to the President's House.

Two years after the start of the War of 1812, British soldiers set fire to the President's House. All that was left standing were the outside walls. After the house was rebuilt, the outside walls were painted white to cover up the fire's black marks. From that time on, it was known as the White House.

Through the years many changes have been made to the White House. Stately porches, terraces, and wings have been added. The entire structure was strengthened with concrete and steel in between 1948 and 1952.

Find Out More

. . . in a Book

Ghosts of the White House by Cheryl Harness (Simon & Schuster Children's, 1997) A young schoolgirl gets her own imaginary tour of the White House led by George Washington, who takes her from room to room, introducing her to past presidents.

. . . on the Web

http://www.whitehouse.gov/WH/kids/html/home.html— Tour the White House with Socks the Cat.

Presidential Plate

Each president generally had a special design of china made for use during his administration.

What You Need

- paper
- pencil
- white glazed ceramic plate
- ceramic paint such as Delta Air-Dry PermEnamel ™
- paintbrush

What To Do

1. Trace around the plate onto a piece of paper.

2. On the paper "plate," draw a design you like.

3. Paint your design onto the ceramic plate with the ceramic paint (found at craft stores).

4. Follow the manufacturer's directions for curing the paint.

Presidents and First Ladies

Match each first lady to her husband, the president (page 103). Some of the names may be used more than once. Two presidents were married twice while in office.

Note: Not all the presidents are listed because they were not all married while in office. Answers are on page 104.

First Ladies' First Names

Louisa	Eliza	Bess	Elizabeth
Letitia	Margaret	Jacqueline	Ellen
Martha	Abigail	Helen	Lady Bird
Dolley	Jane	Sarah	Barbara
Florence	Mary	Anna	Eleanor
Patricia	Lucretia	Nancy	Julia
Rosalynn	Caroline	Mamie	Edith
Lucy	Hillary	Frances	
Ida	Grace	Lou	

Presidents and First Ladies (cont.)

On the lines, write the name of the presidents' wives, or first ladies. Answers are on page 104.

Presidents

George Washington _____

John Adams _____

James Madison _____

James Monroe _____

John Quincy Adams _____

William Henry Harrison _____

John Tyler _____, _____

James Polk _____

Zachary Taylor _____

Millard Fillmore _____

Franklin Pierce _____

Abraham Lincoln _____

Andrew Johnson _____

Ulysses S. Grant _____

Rutherford B. Hayes _____

James Garfield _____

Grover Cleveland _____

Benjamin Harrison _____

William McKinley _____

Theodore Roosevelt _____

William Taft _____

Woodrow Wilson _____, _____

Warren Harding _____

Calvin Coolidge _____

Herbert Hoover _____

Franklin Roosevelt _____

Harry S Truman _____

Dwight D. Eisenhower _____

John F. Kennedy _____

Lyndon B. Johnson _____

Richard Nixon _____

Gerald Ford _____

Jimmy Carter _____

Ronald Reagan _____

George Bush _____

Bill Clinton _____

Presidents and First Ladies *(cont.)*

Answers

Washington—Martha

John Adams—Abigail

Madison—Dolley

Monroe—Elizabeth

John Quincy Adams—Louisa

W.H. Harrison—Anna

Tyler—Letitia and Julia

Polk—Sarah

Taylor—Margaret

Fillmore—Abigail

Pierce—Jane

Lincoln—Mary

Andrew Johnson—Eliza

Grant—Julia

Hayes—Lucy

Garfield—Lucretia

Cleveland—Frances

B. Harrison—Caroline

McKinley—Ida

Theodore Roosevelt—Edith

Taft—Helen

Wilson—Ellen and Edith

Harding—Florence

Coolidge—Grace

Hoover—Lou

Franklin Roosevelt—Eleanor

Truman—Bess

Eisenhower—Mamie

Kennedy—Jacqueline

Lyndon Johnson—Claudia (Lady Bird)

Nixon—Patricia

Ford—Elizabeth

Carter—Rosalynn

Reagan—Nancy

Bush—Barbara

Clinton—Hillary

Mount Rushmore

In the Black Hills of South Dakota is a spectacular creation in the granite cliff of Mount Rushmore. It is a carving of the heads of four great men who also served as presidents of the United States—George Washington, Thomas Jefferson, Theodore Roosevelt, and Abraham Lincoln.

Doane Robinson, state historian of South Dakota, had the idea of making a gigantic sculpture in the Black Hills. He invited sculptor Gutzon Borglum to the Black Hills to see if it could be done. Borglum was intrigued and took the job. Work began on August 10, 1927. On the same day, President Calvin Coolidge declared Mount Rushmore a National Memorial. Borglum died in 1941; his son, Lincoln, finished the carving. It took 14 years.

Each man carved into Mount Rushmore symbolizes something that makes America great. Washington stands for the struggle for independence and the birth of our nation. Jefferson represents the ideal of government of the people, by the people, and for the people. Lincoln symbolizes the struggle for equality, and Roosevelt the conscience and influence of 20th-century America.

Find Out More

. . . on the Web

http://www.state.sd.us/tourism/rushmore/album.htm—This site features several photographs of Mount Rushmore with links to the history of its creation.

Personal Memorial Paperweight

What You Need

- plasticine clay
- plastic knife
- toothpick

What To Do

1. Choose three or four people important in your life for your memorial.

2. Shape the clay into a "mountain cliff."

3. Roll a small ball of clay for each person in your memorial and press them into the side of the cliff.

4. Make facial features by pinching, pulling, and carving with the knife and toothpick.

5. Carve with the toothpick the name of each person at the base of the memorial.

6. Let the memorial dry and use it as a paperweight.

Note: You can paint the memorial after it has dried to resemble granite by giving it a base coat of gray and then flicking darker gray, white, and black paint on it with a toothbrush.

Iwo Jima Memorial

Iwo Jima is a small island south of Tokyo, Japan. Mount Suribachi, an extinct volcano, rises 550 feet at the southern tip of the island. One of the most famous incidents of World War II happened on top of Mount Suribachi, an incident that captured the hearts of Americans and was immortalized in bronze at the Marine Corps War Memorial.

In 1945, the United States was trying to end the war in the Pacific. They had recaptured most of the territory taken by the Japanese in 1941 and 1942. Iwo Jima, however, was still under Japanese control. On February 19, the United States Marines invaded Iwo Jima and were ordered to capture Mount Suribachi. By February 21, they had reached the base of the mountain, and the next day they surrounded it.

On February 23, Marines placed a small American flag at the mountain's summit. That afternoon the little flag was replaced with a large one raised by five Marines and a Navy hospital corpsman. The raising of this flag was photographed by Joe Rosenthal, who won a Pulitzer Prize for the image.

Felix W. de Weldon constructed a scale model and then a life-size model of the men triumphantly raising the flag. The statue was first completed in plaster and then cast in bronze, a process that took three years. On the base of the statue is a tribute to the fighting men on Iwo Jima: "Uncommon Valor was a Common Virtue."

Find Out More

. . . on the Web

http://www.co.arlington.va/us/arlcty/gallery/iwojima.htm—This site includes closeup photos of the memorial as well as a link to the United States Marine Corps.

Ellis Island

For hundreds of years, people from other countries have come to the United States, seeking freedom in this land of promise. Over 12 million of these immigrants were processed through a tiny island in New York Harbor—Ellis Island.

The island served as an immigration station for over 60 years. It opened as a reception center in 1892. In 1897 the wooden buildings burned and were replaced by a castle-like structure in 1900. This was used to process immigrants until 1943, when New York City took on these duties.

Immigrants went through several steps when they arrived at Ellis Island. They entered the main building and checked in their baggage. They were given a "six-second medical" and checked for contagious diseases. If the doctor suspected serious problems, an "X" was written in chalk on the person's clothing. This guaranteed him or her a return trip home.

Those who passed the medical inspection moved into the Registry Room, where their legal documents were checked. They were asked questions by the inspectors. Those who passed were allowed into the ticket office to buy tickets to the places they wanted to go. Those who were detained were housed in rooms in the main building and fed meals in the dining room. About one out of every six people was delayed for as long as four days because of medical problems.

Ellis Island *(cont.)*

During the peak years of immigration, the center processed up to 10,000 immigrants a day, although it was only designed to handle 5,000. Immigration laws were put into effect in the 1920s, and the flood of people gradually dwindled. In 1954 Ellis Island was closed. Over the years, the structures there became ruined by time and vandalism.

In 1965, Ellis Island became part of the Statue of Liberty National Monument. As more and more people became interested in their family histories and origins, interest in Ellis Island revived. Beginning in the 1980s, a gigantic

restoration effort began. The original structure and character of Ellis Island have now been restored.

On September 10, 1990, the Ellis Island Immigration Museum opened. Pictures and exhibits help re-create for visitors the experience of the immigrants who arrived as "huddled masses yearning to breathe free."

Find Out More

. . . in a Book

Elisabeth by Claire Nivola (Ferrar, Straus and Giroux, 1997). This is the touching true story of a young girl who has to flee for her life to America, leaving behind everything that is precious to her, including her beloved doll.

When Jessie Came Across the Sea by Amy Hest (Candlewick Press, 1997).

Do People Grow on Family Trees? by Ira Wolfman (Workman Publishing, 1991). This is a great resource for becoming an "ancestor detector."

. . . on the Web

http://www.i-channel.com/ellis/index.html—This site contains photos and audio clips of remembrances of people who were processed through Ellis Island.

Family History

What You Need

- tape recorder
- blank tape
- pencil
- paper
- relatives

What To Do

Choose an older relative, and ask if it's all right if you tape-record his or her answers to some questions about your family. Then interview others in the same family to see whether they have different memories and/or feelings about the same events.

Make a list of questions you want to ask, such as the following:

- What is your full name?
- Were you named after anyone?
- When were you born?
- If you weren't born in the United States, when did you arrive here?
- What are your parents' names?
- What are the names of your brothers and sisters?
- What countries/states/cities did you grow up in?
- What do you remember about the house you grew up in?
- What do you remember most about your childhood?

Native Americans

Native American Food

Great Plains tribes made their soup in cleaned and emptied buffalo paunches, or stomachs. Northwest tribes made their soups in cedar boxes, and California tribes made theirs in tightly woven baskets. Stones were heated in a fire and then dropped into the soup container with water, meat, and vegetables. The hot rocks would cook the soup.

Native Americans had to store much food. Fish and meat were cut into strips and dried in the sun or smoked over a fire. Apples and other fruits and berries were dried in the sun. Food was stored in baskets, pottery jars, leather pouches, or wooden boxes.

Pemmican, a favorite food of many Native Americans, was made from dried meat (buffalo, caribou, or deer), crushed berries and nuts, and animal fat. The meat and berry mixture was paced in a rawhide bag about the size of a pillowcase. Hot fat was poured into the bag and the bag sewn shut. Then people walked on the bag to flatten it. These flat bags of pemmican would harden when they cooled, and the food inside would last for many years.

Find Out More

. . . on the Web

http://www.lib.uconn.edu/NativeTech/food/—This site offers a good collection of Native American recipes.

Native Americans were hunters, gatherers, and farmers. They had to find or grow their own food to survive. Different people cooked in different ways. Open pits were dug in the ground and lined with stones. Then a fire was started in the pit. Some foods were wrapped in cornhusks or leaves and cooked under hot ashes.

Fruit Leather

What You Need

- 2 cups (500 mL) of ripe fruit (apricots, plums, apples, peaches, or strawberries)
- kitchen knife
- blender
- spoon
- cookie sheet
- plastic wrap

What To Do

1. Wash and drain the fruit. Cut it into small chunks.

2. Chop the fruit in a blender for about 15 seconds.

3. Line a cookie sheet with plastic wrap.

4. Pour the blended fruit onto the plastic wrap and let it dry.

Pemmican

What You Need

- 1 package of beef jerky
- ½ cup (125 mL) raisins
- 2 tablespoons (30 mL) brown sugar
- up to ½ cup (125 mL) berries (any kind) and ground nuts (optional)
- oil, melted butter, or melted suet
- blender
- bowl
- spoon
- 9" x 11" (23 cm x 28 cm) cake pan
- knife
- spatula
- resealable sandwich bags

What To Do

1. Mince the jerky in the blender until it is in small pieces.

2. Add raisins, berries, and nuts. Blend just long enough to break up berries.

3. Put the mixture in a bowl and stir in the sugar and enough melted fat to make the mixture stick together.

4. Pat the mixture into the cake pan and let it cool and harden.

5. Cut the pemmican into bars and store it in resealable plastic bags.

Note: If you use suet (available from the butcher), these bars will keep for several months.

Parfleche

A parfleche is a rawhide "folder" used to carry pemmican.

What You Need

- pencil
- brown paper grocery sack
- scissors
- crayons
- yarn

What To Do

1. Trace a parfleche pattern onto the paper bag.

2. Cut out the parfleche and decorate it with crayons.

3. Fold the sides together and then fold the top and bottom in towards the middle.

4. Slip in a treat (wrapped in plastic) and tie a piece of yarn around the parfleche to keep it closed.

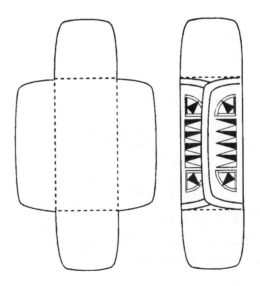

Animals in Life and Legend

Animals have always been important to Native Americans. In the past, animals provided meat to eat, furs for clothing and bedding, and hides for shelter and bags. Bones, teeth, antlers, feathers, and claws were used for tools, weapons, and jewelry, as well as for ceremonial objects.

Animals were believed to act as guides and protectors of humans. They often appeared in dreams or in people's waking visions. When a certain animal appeared in a dream, that animal was considered to be a totem, or a spirit helper, of the dreamer. The person may have painted the animal on his tipi, blanket, or leather shield. In the Northwest, tribes carved wooden totem poles showing animals and humans.

Fetishes are objects that many Native Americans believed to have special or magical powers. Most fetishes are carved in the shapes of animals and are made from shell, coral, turquoise, jet, mother of pearl, clay, or sandstone. The Zuni people of the Southwest are famous for their carved fetishes.

Native Americans of the Great Plains and Southwest discovered horses when they were brought to the New World by the Spaniards. Horses became a very important part of Native American life. People rode horses, used them to transport their belongings, and traded them instead of using money. Artists drew horses on buffalo hide robes and the walls of caves.

Find Out More

. . . in a Book

The Girl Who Loved Wild Horses by Paul Goble (Simon and Schuster, 1993).

Storm Boy by Paul Owen Lewis (Beyond Words Publishing, 1995). A Haida boy enters the realm of the Killer Whale people.

Mystery of the Navajo Moon by Timothy Green (Northland Publishing, 1991, 1993).

Clay Fetish

What You Need

- plasticine clay (like Sculpey®)
- round toothpick
- leather thong, string, or yarn

What To Do

1. Form the clay into an animal shape.

2. Use the toothpick to etch in details such as eyes and mouth.

3. With the toothpick, poke a hole through the animal. Allow the shape to dry, or bake it according to package directions.

4. When the animal is dry, thread the leather thong through the hole and tie it around your neck.

5. You may wish to tie beads and feathers onto your animal for decoration.

Draw a Horse

Use the steps below to draw a horse on a separate sheet of paper. Color your horse in a Native American scene.

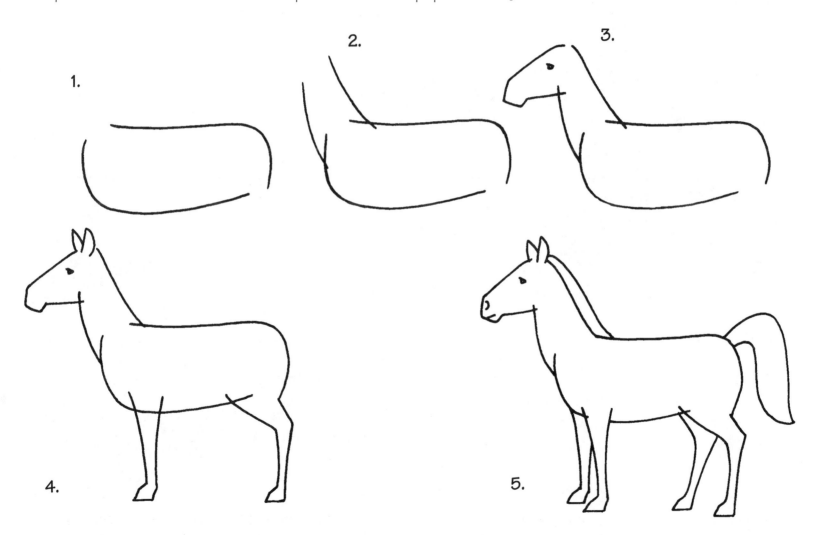

1.

2.

3.

4.

5.

Dance and Drama

Native Americans were grateful for the many things nature provided them. One way they gave thanks was with special dances. Rain cycles, moon cycles, planting and harvesting times, and the migrations of animals such as deer, bison, and salmon were celebrated with days and nights of feasting, storytelling, singing, prayers, dance, and music.

Dance dramas entertained the people and taught them how to live in peace with animals, plants, and other people. By watching the dances, children learned the stories of their ancestors. The singers and dancers often wore makeup, masks, large headpieces, and colorful costumes.

The dancers were accompanied by many different kinds of musical instruments such as rattles made from hollow gourds, wooden flutes, and bells made from shells. Drums were made from hollow logs, animal skins, and baskets. Dancers carried dancing shields of painted rawhide. Many tribes believed the earth was built on the back of a giant turtle. The Cherokee called the earth "Turtle Island." The turtle was a favorite shape for the rattles used in dance ceremonies.

Find Out More

. . . in a Book

Beardream by Will Hobbs (Simon and Schuster Children's, 1997). Short Tail, a Ute boy, has a bear dream and shows his people the Bear Dance to celebrate the end of winter and the awakening of the bears.

Dancing with the Indians by Angela Shelf Medearis (Holiday House, 1991, 1993). This book depicts Seminole dancing celebrations.

. . . on the Web

http://homel.gte.net/wolfdanc/—Visit this page to hear authentic Native American drums and singers.

Ceremonial Dancing Shield

What You Need

- cardboard circle, about 14" (35 cm) in diameter
- yarn, ribbon, or raffia
- feathers
- tape
- paints
- paintbrush
- scissors
- beads
- hole punch

What To Do

1. Paint a design on one side of the circle.

2. Tape a handle to the back.

3. Punch holes around the bottom half of the circle.

4. Thread pieces of yarn, ribbon, or raffia through each hole and then thread two or three beads on each piece of yarn.

5. Tie a feather to each piece of yarn.

Hand Drum

What You Need

- oatmeal box
- construction paper
- glue or tape
- paint
- paintbrush
- wooden spoon
- feathers
- yarn or raffia

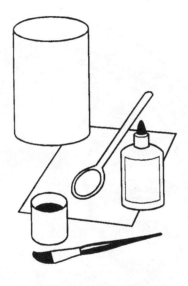

What To Do

1. Glue or tape paper around the oatmeal box.

2. Paint Native American designs on the side of the drum and on the wooden spoon.

3. When the paint is dry, tie feathers onto the drumstick and the sides of the drum with yarn or raffia.

Turtle Rattle

What You Need

- 2 small paper plates
- ½ cup (125 mL) dried beans
- paper towel tube
- paint
- paintbrushes
- stapler
- scissors
- glue

What To Do

1. Draw and paint a turtle shell design on the back of both paper plates.

2. Paint the paper towel tube.

3. Staple the fronts of the paper plates together. Before you finish stapling, put the beans inside.

4. Cut two slits across from each other in the paper towel tube.

5. Slide the rattle into the slits and glue it into place.

Basket Weaving and Pottery

shoulder straps were carried by farmers and food gatherers as they harvested corn, roots, acorns, or cactus fruit.

Woven baby carriers were made of grasses and lined with soft moss or fur. Special cooking baskets were tightly woven and coated on the inside with pine tree sap to make them waterproof. Birchbark baskets were used for storage and carrying food and household things and as "hot stone" cooking pots.

Pottery was also used in many different ways. Clay pots were used for carrying and storing food, seeds, and dry grains. Clay canteens and bottles were used to carry and store water. The people of the Southeast and Southwest made pottery dishes, plates, pipes, cups, pots, and bottles. The nomadic tribes of the Great Plains did not make pots because they were heavy and breakable, and the tribes of the Northwest used wooden boxes instead of clay pots.

Find Out More

. . . on the Web

http://www.libuconn.edu/NativeTech/coil/coiinstr.html—You can find detailed instructions for making a coiled pine needle basket at this site.

Early Native Americans used all sorts of baskets to carry and store food, seeds, water, and household things. Flat basket trays were used for drying food in the sun. Special baskets were made for gathering shellfish and as nets to catch salmon.

In the Southwest, special basket drums were used in healing ceremonies. Seed baskets had small openings that made it easier to pour out the tiny seeds and helped keep mice from climbing inside. Large baskets with

Woven Basket

What You Need

- tall wild grass
- raffia
- darning needle
- scissors

What To Do

1. Lay three or four strands of grass together and tie with raffia at 1½" (3.84 cm) intervals.

2. When you get near the ends of the strands, lay down three or four more strands, overlapping the ends to form a long rope. Continue overlapping and tying until your rope is at least 36" (91 cm) long.

3. Thread the needle with raffia.

4. Coil the rope in a spiral pattern and stitch with raffia to hold it in place.

5. Continue coiling and stitching, gradually building up the sides of the basket as you go.

Note: This would make a good partner project. One person could wrap while the other person began coiling and stitching the other end.

Birchbark Basket

What You Need

- cardboard
- white and brown paint
- paintbrush
- black or brown crayon
- scissors
- sharp pencil
- ruler
- yarn or leather thong

What To Do

1. Draw and cut out a pattern on the cardboard.

2. Paint the outside of the basket white, let it dry, and add black or brown lines with crayon to make it look like birchbark. Paint on designs with brown paint.

3. Punch holes at each corner with a sharp pencil.

4. Using the tip of the scissors and the ruler, score the unpainted side of the cardboard along the dotted lines on the pattern.

5. Fold the sides up to form a basket.

6. Thread a leather thong or yarn through the holes to tie the corners together.

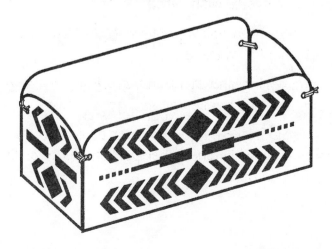

#2361 Hooray for the USA!

Clay Coil Pot

What You Need

- soft clay
- water
- newspaper (to work on)

What To Do

1. Form a small slab of clay for the base of your coil pot.

2. Take a large handful of moist clay and squeeze it into an oval shape.

3. Using both hands, roll the oval into a long coil. Repeat steps two and three several times.

4. Attach the coils to the slab and press them together.

5. After the coils have been built up as high as you like, smooth the coils with your fingers after dipping them in water.

6. Use your finger to carve your pot with patterns or pictures. Let it dry.

Communication

Over 30 dialects were spoken by Native Americans who lived on the Great Plains. Picture symbols were painted on a buffalo hide each winter to record important events that had happened during the year. This was called a winter count. Picture symbols were also used to tell stories, send messages, and decorate tipis and clothing.

Native Americans believed that the Great Spirit communicated to them through dreams and visions. Dream catchers were woven hoops hung over a child's bed or cradleboard. They are said to have originated with the Oneida in the northeastern United States. The hoops were decorated with shells, feathers, beads, and ribbons. Bad dreams were "captured" by the dream catcher, but good dreams passed through to the sleeper.

Find Out More

. . . in a Book

Native American Tales and Activities by Mari Lu Robbins (Teacher Created Materials, 1996). This book contains a variety of myths and legends from several different groups.

Dreamcatcher by Audrey Osofsky (Orchard Books Watts, 1992).

People have always needed a way to communicate with each other. In the past, Native Americans across the country spoke more than 600 dialects based on seven major language groups. How did Native Americans speak to each other and to other tribes? How did they keep a record of their history and their stories? When people from different areas met together to trade or for special celebrations, they had to communicate some other way. That way was usually sign language.

Make a Winter Count

What You Need

- brown paper grocery sack
- pencil
- paint
- paintbrushes

What To Do

1. Tear the paper bag on the folds and open it up to lay flat.

2. Lightly trace the shape of a buffalo hide on the sack and then tear out the shape, following your line.

3. Starting in the center and spiraling outward, paint pictographs that reflect the important things that have happened in your life.

4. Share your winter count with others.

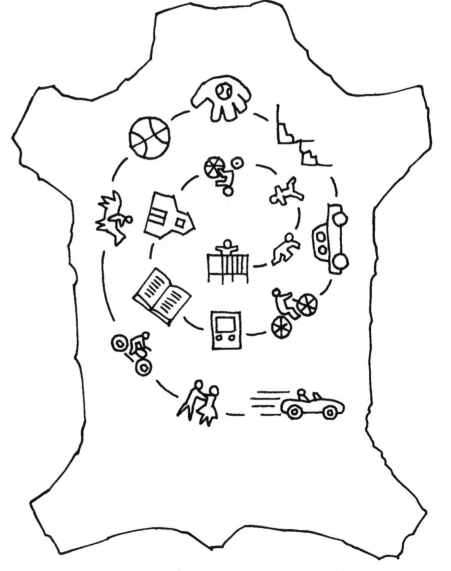

Dream Catcher

What You Need

- wire clothes hanger
- string, yarn, ribbon, or leather thong
- beads
- feathers

What To Do

1. Bend the hanger into a hoop.

2. Tie one end of the string or yarn to the hoop. Wrap the string around the hoop at even intervals.

3. When you have gone around the entire circle, start the next set of wraps in the center of the first wrap made. Keep the string pulled snug.

4. Continue around until only a small circle remains open in the center of the hoop. Tie off the string.

5. Tie feathers and string beads on short lengths of yarn and then tie the yarn to your dream catcher.

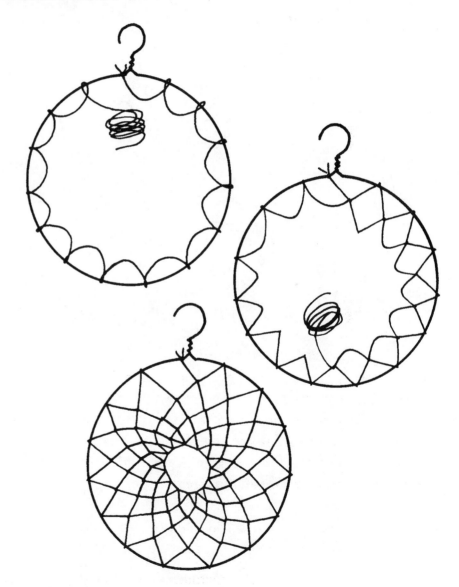

Clothing and Jewelry

Native Americans of the past had to make their own clothes from materials they found in nature. Native Americans in the Far North used animal skins and furs. In the hot Southwest and Southeast, clothes were made of woven plant fibers. On the Great Plains, the clothing changed with the season. Needles were made from animal bones, and sinew (animal tendon) or plant fiber was used for thread. It required great skill and patience to prepare the skin or weave the fiber, sew or weave the clothes, and decorate them with paint, quills, beads, or shells.

Many other useful items were woven, including rugs, blankets, sashes, dresses, carrying bags, and hats. Both plant fibers (grass, cotton, bark) and animal fibers (hair from goats, dogs, moose, caribou, and sheep) were used. In the Southwest, wool was spun into yarn on a spindle and then woven on a wooden loom.

Jewelry was made from local materials, such as seeds, shells, and animal bones, as well as from traded items. Shells such as cowrie, clams, and abalone from coastal regions were traded for such things as porcupine quills from the north. Feathers, animal teeth and hair, claws, antlers, ivory, stones, and fur were used for jewelry and clothing decoration.

Find Out More

. . . in a Book

Mama, Do You Love Me? by Barbara Joosse (Chronicle Books, 1991). This tale of a mother and her child showcases the culture of the far north.

. . . on the Web

http:www.lib.uconn.edu/NativeTech/clothing/moccasin/mocinstr.html—Find out how to create center-seam moccasins; included are a pattern and instructions.

Weaving

What You Need

- 4" x 12" (10 cm x 30 cm) cardboard rectangle
- scissors
- yarn
- tape
- pencil

What To Do

1. Cut small notches along the top and bottom edges of the cardboard loom about ½" (1.3 cm) apart.

2. Wrap yarn through each notch. Tape the ends of the yarn to the loom. This is the warp.

3. Tape one end of a long piece of yarn to the pencil. Use the pencil like a needle to thread the yarn through the warp, weaving over and under. When you run out of yarn or want to change yarn colors, tie off the ends. This is the weft.

4. Continue weaving until the loom is filled. Cut and tie the warp ends, and remove your weaving from the loom.

Note: You may wish to form this weaving into a pouch. Fold it in thirds, stitch the two bottom thirds together on the sides, and fold the top third down for a flap. Attach the pouch to your belt with yarn, or hang it around your neck.

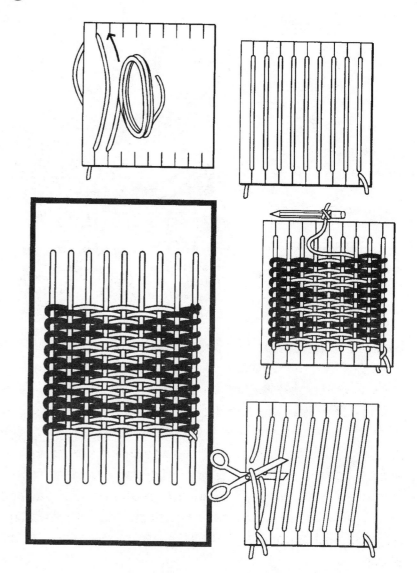

Paper Beads

What You Need

- magazine pages
- scissors
- glue
- wax paper
- thread
- bamboo skewer

What To Do

1. Cut long triangular strips from the magazine pages about 1" (2.54 cm) wide at the base and tapering to a point at the tip.

2. Roll each strip up tightly around the bamboo skewer, starting at the base of the triangle. Each triangle makes one bead.

3. Coat the bead with glue, slide it off the skewer, and set on wax paper to dry.

4. When the beads are dry, string them together on the thread and tie it around your neck.

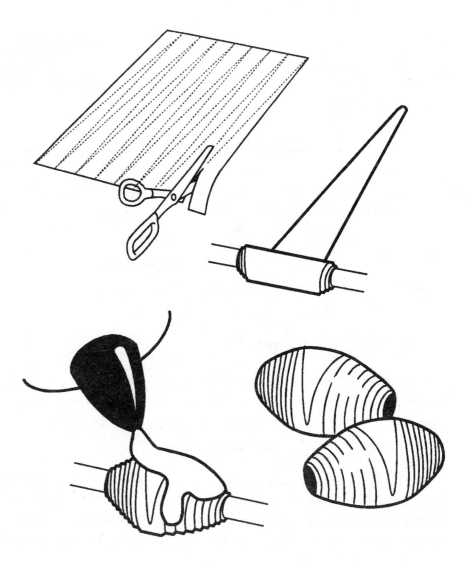

Toys and Games

war" by tribes in the Southeast. Early French settlers named the game lacrosse because the racket looked like a bishop's crosier, or staff. The ball is not to be touched with hands. Instead, the racket is used to pick up the ball, throw it, and carry it into or across a goal.

Many Native Americans enjoyed string games. These games were played by taking a long strip of sinew, leather, or yarn and forming intricate pictures with it. Sometimes a second player pulled the yarn away and formed a new picture. Foot races were also popular. One of the most challenging was an obstacle course race.

Find Out More

. . . in a Book

The Mud Family by Betsy James (G.P. Putnam's Sons, 1994). Sosi, an Anasazi girl, makes toys from mud and solves her family's problem.

. . . on the Web

http://home.eznet/~stevemd/stringar.html—You'll find instructions for making Jacob's Ladder, Two Mountains and a Stream, and Walking Sticks at this site dedicated to string games.

Native American children used sticks, reeds, grass, stones, feathers, and animal hides to make toys. Ball games were popular with Native American children and adults. Balls were made from sewn leather, stones, wood, grass, and rubber.

Lacrosse was a game played with a small ball and a three-foot stick ending in a webbed paddle. This was called "men hit a rounded object" by the Onondaga and "little brother of

Races

Run an Obstacle Course Race

Go with a friend to a large area. Decide on a course, the obstacles you will have to overcome, and the style of racing. For example, you may decide to run around the big tree, skip to the bush, crawl under the bush, hop backwards across the path, and then run backwards to the finish line. With a stopwatch, time each other to see who can complete the course the fastest.

Run a Three-Legged Race

Get at least three other friends and choose partners. Partners tie one of their legs together. Set out a course. See who can run the fastest tied together.

All Around America

State Facts Charts

State	Abbr.	Capital	Statehood	Admission	Nickname
Alabama	AL	Montgomery	1819	22nd	The Heart of Dixie
Alaska	AK	Juneau	1959	49th	The Frontier State
Arizona	AZ	Phoenix	1912	48th	The Grand Canyon State
Arkansas	AR	Little Rock	1836	25th	The Land of Opportunity
California	CA	Sacramento	1850	31st	The Golden State
Colorado	CO	Denver	1876	38th	The Centennial State
Connecticut	CT	Hartford	1788	5th	The Constitution State
Delaware	DE	Dover	1787	1st	The First State
Florida	FL	Tallahassee	1845	27th	The Sunshine State

State Facts Charts (cont.)

State	Abbr.	Capital	Statehood	Admission	Nickname
Georgia	GA	Atlanta	1788	4th	The Empire State of the South
Hawaii	HI	Honolulu	1959	50th	The Aloha State
Idaho	ID	Boise	1890	43rd	The Gem State
Illinois	IL	Springfield	1818	21st	The Prairie State
Indiana	IN	Indianapolis	1816	19th	The Hoosier State
Iowa	IA	Des Moines	1846	29th	The Hawkeye State
Kansas	KS	Topeka	1861	34th	The Sunflower State
Kentucky	KY	Frankfort	1792	15th	The Bluegrass State
Louisiana	LA	Baton Rouge	1812	18th	The Pelican State

State Facts Charts *(cont.)*

State	Abbr.	Capital	Statehood	Admission	Nickname
Maine	ME	Augusta	1820	23rd	The Pine Tree State
Maryland	MD	Annapolis	1788	7th	The Old Line State
Massachusetts	MA	Boston	1788	6th	The Bay State
Michigan	MI	Lansing	1837	26th	The Wolverine State
Minnesota	MN	St. Paul	1858	32nd	The Gopher State
Mississippi	MS	Jackson	1817	20th	The Magnolia State
Missouri	MO	Jefferson City	1821	24th	The Show Me State
Montana	MT	Helena	1889	41st	The Treasure State
Nebraska	NE	Lincoln	1867	37th	The Cornhusker State

State Facts Charts (cont.)

State	Abbr.	Capital	Statehood	Admission	Nickname
Nevada	NV	Carson City	1864	36th	The Silver State
New Hampshire	NH	Concord	1788	9th	The Granite State
New Jersey	NJ	Trenton	1787	3rd	The Garden State
New Mexico	NM	Santa Fe	1912	47th	The Land of Enchantment
New York	NY	Albany	1788	11th	The Empire State
North Carolina	NC	Raleigh	1789	12th	The Tar Heel State
North Dakota	ND	Bismarck	1889	39th	The Flickertail State
Ohio	OH	Columbus	1803	17th	The Buckeye State
Oklahoma	OK	Oklahoma City	1907	46th	The Sooner State

State Facts Charts *(cont.)*

State	Abbr.	Capital	Statehood	Admission	Nickname
Oregon	OR	Salem	1859	33rd	The Beaver State
Pennsylvania	PA	Harrisburg	1787	2nd	The Keystone State
Rhode Island	RI	Providence	1790	13th	The Ocean State
South Carolina	SC	Columbia	1788	8th	The Palmetto State
South Dakota	SD	Pierre	1889	40th	The Sunshine State
Tennessee	TN	Nashville	1796	16th	The Volunteer State
Texas	TX	Austin	1845	28th	The Lone Star State
Utah	UT	Salt Lake City	1859	45th	The Beehive State
Vermont	VT	Montpelier	1791	14th	The Green Mountain State

State Facts Charts *(cont.)*

State	Abbr.	Capital	Statehood	Admission	Nickname
Virginia	VA	Richmond	1788	10th	Old Dominion
Washington	WA	Olympia	1889	42nd	The Evergreen State
West Virginia	WV	Charleston	1863	35th	The Mountain State
Wisconsin	WI	Madison	1848	30th	The Badger State
Wyoming	WY	Cheyenne	1890	44th	The Equality State

East and Northeast States Trivia

Research to find which state correctly completes each sentence. Write the state name on the line. Answers are on pages 154–155.

1. Phineas Taylor Barnum was born in _____.
   He opened his first circus in 1871 and later joined
   with James Bailey to create "The Greatest Show on
   Earth."

2. Home to Ethan Allen and the Green Mountain Boys,
   _____ is one of three states in
   the U.S. that were independent republics before
   becoming states.

3. The first beauty contest was held in _____
   at Rehoboth Beach in 1880. It was named "Miss
   United States," and one of the judges was Thomas
   Edison.

4. Francis Scott Key wrote "The Star-Spangled
   Banner" in _____ during the War of 1812.

5. Thomas Edison invented the electric light bulb and
   phonograph in his laboratory in Menlo Park in
   _____.

6. _____ was the first colony to claim
   independence from Britain in May of 1776.

7. The World Trade Center, located in _____, is
   so large that each of the twin towers has separate
   zip codes.

8. The world's largest chocolate factory is located in
   _____ in a town named Hershey.

9. Three U.S. presidents were born in _____,
   all named John: John Adams, John Quincy Adams,
   and John F. Kennedy.

10. _____ is the smallest state, 475
    of which could fit into Alaska, the largest state.

11. _____ leads the country in
    production of maple syrup.

12. More toothpicks are produced in _____
    than anywhere else in the United States.

13. Baseball's first World Series was played in
    _____ in October of 1903.

14. Horace Greeley, founder of the New York Tribune, was
    born in Amherst, _____, in 1811.
    Many people followed his famous advice to "Go West,
    young man, and grow up with the country."

15. _____ is home to Atlantic City,
    real-life setting for the game of Monopoly®.

East and Northeast States Map

South and Southeast States Trivia

Research to find which state correctly completes each sentence. Write the state name on the line. Answers are on pages 154–155.

1. George Washington Carver gained a reputation as one of the world's greatest agricultural scientists from the research he completed at Tuskegee University in _____. He found more than 300 uses for the peanut plant and its fruit.

2. Bill Clinton, born in _____ and once its governor, became president of the United States in 1993.

3. Juliette Gordon Low founded the Girl Scouts of America on March 12, 1912, in _____.

4. _____ has more lakes than any other state in the U.S. Lake Okechobee, the second largest freshwater lake completely within the United States' borders, is here.

5. Coca Cola was first served in a drugstore in _____.

6. Louis Armstrong, from _____, was a famous American jazz trumpet player known for his musical abilities and his special singing style.

7. Davy Crockett was a famous frontiersman from _____. He was an expert marksman and served in the Congress.

8. The United States Gold Depository is in _____.

9. Tabasco sauce originated on Avery Island, _____.

10. Elvis Presley, a rock and roll music legend, was born in _____.

11. Eight U.S. Presidents were born in _____. They were Washington, Jefferson, Madison, Monroe, Harrison, Tyler, Taylor, and Wilson.

12. The world's first human heart transplant was in _____ in 1964.

13. The Wright brothers completed the world's first airplane flight in _____ in 1903.

14. More Revolutionary War battles were fought in _____ than any other state.

15. General "Stonewall" Jackson, a famous Confederate military leader, was born and raised on a farm called Jackson's Mill in _____.

South and Southeast States Map

Midwest States Research Quiz

Research to find which state correctly completes each sentence. Write the state name on the line. Answers are on pages 154–155.

1. The first United States kindergarten was opened in Watertown, _____, in 1856.

2. The faces of four U.S. presidents are carved on the side of a mountain in the Black Hills of _____.

3. Eight U.S. presidents have come from _____. They are Grant, Garfield, Hayes, McKinley, Harding, Taft, William Harrison, and Benjamin Harrison.

4. Ice-cream cones were first served here at the 1904 World's Fair in St. Louis, _____.

5. In the late 1800s, Henry Ford used assembly lines at his Detroit factory in _____ to manufacture cars that were affordable for the average American.

6. Grant Wood, an American artist known for his paintings of the Midwest, was born in _____. One of his most famous works is "American Gothic," which shows a serious-looking farm couple.

7. Abraham Lincoln practiced law in _____ before being elected president in 1860.

8. In 1826, New Harmony, _____, became the first city to teach girls and boys together in the same classes.

9. Amelia Earhart, born in Atchison, _____, was the first woman pilot to fly an airplane solo across the Atlantic Ocean. Her historic flight took place in 1932.

10. Duluth, _____, is the busiest freshwater port in the United States.

11. The geographic center of North America is located in _____.

12. _____ was opened up for settlement in 1889 in a famous "Land Run." Those who sneaked over the border to stake claims before the appointed time were called Sooners.

13. A third of the houses in a large city in _____ were burned in the Great Fire of 1871. A cow was believed to have started the fire when it knocked over a lantern.

14. Native sons of _____ include Gerald Ford, Red Cloud, Crazy Horse, Fred Astair, Henry Fonda, and Johnny Carson.

15. Cowboy and humorist Will Rogers is from _____. He gave lectures, did rope tricks, and worked in both the political and business world. He is most famous for saying, "I never met a man I didn't like."

Midwest States Map

Southwest States Trivia

Research to find which state correctly completes each sentence. Write the state name on the line. Answers are on pages 154–155.

1. Rainbow Bridge National Monument in _____ preserves the largest known natural bridge. The pinkish arch stands 309 feet high.

2. _____ leads the nation in producing oil, provides one third of the oil produced in the U.S., and produces more than one third of the nation's natural gas.

3. The first organized rodeo was held in _____ in Prescott on July 4, 1888. It was called a Cowboy Tournament.

4. The Smokey Bear Historical State Park is located in Capitan, _____. A little bear was found clinging to a tree during a forest fire, and Smokey the Bear became a symbol to help prevent forest fires.

5. "Remember the Alamo!" became a battlecry during the Mexican War. The restored fort is now a national park in _____.

6. _____ receives the least amount of rainfall of all the states in the U.S.

7. The Great Salt Lake, located in _____, is four times saltier than any ocean.

8. The United States government owns more than three-fourths of the land in _____.

9. Two U.S. presidents were born in _____. They are Dwight D. Eisenhower and Lyndon B. Johnson.

10. The Golden Spike Ceremony, celebrated in Promontory, _____, on May 10, 1869, marked the joining of the Central Pacific and the Union Pacific, creating the nation's first transcontinental railroad.

11. Sandra Day O'Connor was the first woman to be appointed to the Supreme Court of the United States. This historic event took place in 1981. She was born in Texas but was a resident of and served in the state senate and as a judge for the Supreme Court of _____.

12. Bill Mauldin, a cartoonist from _____, became famous for his realistic cartoons of army life during World War II, which featured his cartoon character GI Joe.

13. Sam Houston fought for the independence of _____ from Mexico.

14. Nearly $750 million of silver and gold was mined over the course of 30 years in the mining town of Virginia City, _____.

15. Brigham Young led a group of Mormons west across the young United States in search of religious freedom. He and his followers arrived and settled in _____ on July 24, 1847.

Southwest States Map

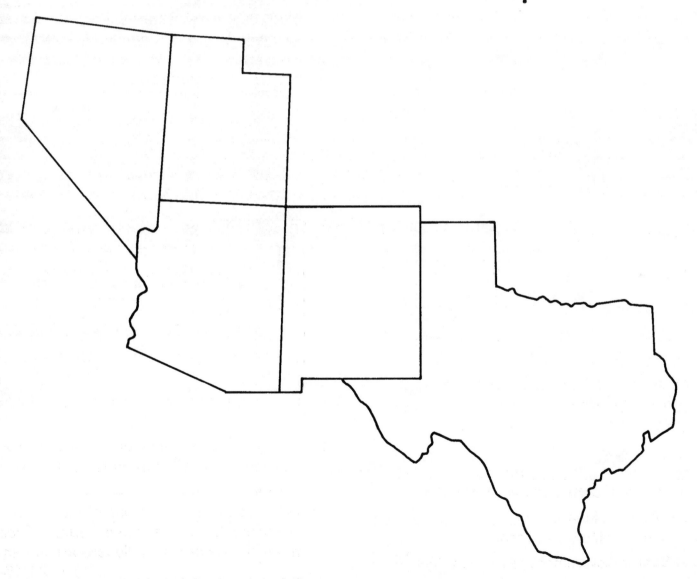

Mountain States Trivia

Research to find which state correctly completes each sentence. Write the state name on the line. Answers are on pages 154–155.

1. The largest silver nugget was discovered in Aspen, _____ in 1894. It weighed 1,840 pounds.

2. Jim Bridger was a mountain man who crossed the mountain states several times. He and a partner established Fort Bridger in _____, on the Oregon Trail.

3. _____ is the potato capital of the United States. It produces over 10 billion pounds of potatoes each year.

4. Buffalo Bill Cody, originally from Iowa, had a colorful career as a Pony Express rider, Union Army scout, sharpshooter, guide, and hunter. His Wild West shows popularized and romanticized images of the Old West. He is buried on Lookout Mountain in _____.

5. More sapphires are found in _____ than anywhere else in the United States.

6. South Pass, a famous mountain pass at the southern end of the Wind River Range of _____, was used by pioneers to cross the Continental Divide.

7. Jeannette Rankin was the first woman in the United States Congress. She was elected in 1916 from _____.

8. Electricity from atomic energy was first generated in _____, and in 1955 the village of Arco was the first in the U.S. to be lighted for one hour by nuclear power.

9. The dome of the capitol building of _____ is covered with gold leaf that was mined locally.

10. Lieutenant Colonel George A. Custer, leader of the Seventh Cavalry, was defeated in _____ by the Sioux in 1876, in a battle known as Custer's Last Stand.

11. Grasshopper Glacier, near Cooke City, _____, is named for the grasshoppers that became trapped in the ice thousands of years ago and can still be seen today.

12. Independence Rock, a large granite boulder located near Casper, _____, has names carved in it by pioneers who were moving west during the 1800s.

13. Jack Dempsey, winner of the world heavyweight title in 1919, was called the "Manassa Mauler" after his birthplace of Manassa, _____.

14. Chief Joseph, the leader of the Nez Perce Indians of _____, was known as a great leader and humanitarian who worked for peace.

Mountain States Map

Pacific and Northwest States Trivia

Research to find which state correctly completes each sentence. Write the state name on the line. Answers are on pages 154–155.

1. The greatest snowfall recorded in one year in North America occurred in _____ between July 1971 and June 1972. A total of 1,122 inches of snow fell.

2. Japan attacked _____ by air on December 7, 1941. During the attack the USS Arizona sank with more than 1,000 men aboard. A floating memorial now rests over the hull of the battleship.

3. Father Junipero Serra founded a string of missions along the coast of _____ in the 1700s.

4. Gold was discovered in _____ in 1880.

5. The world's oldest tree, the General Sherman, located in _____, is about 2,500 years old.

6. One of the world's largest inactive volcanoes is located in _____. It measures about 25 miles around the rim.

7. The world's smallest official park is found in _____. The park covers an area of 452 square inches.

8. Linus Pauling, winner of two Nobel prizes, was born in _____.

9. _____ is the only state in the nation to be named after a president.

10. Lewis and Clark reached the Pacific Coast in November 1805 and camped for the winter at Fort Clatsop, _____.

11. More bald eagles nest along the Chilkat River in _____ than anywhere else in the world.

12. The first cable-car street system was introduced in _____ in 1873.

13. The alphabet of the native people of _____ only has twelve letters—a, e, h, i, k, l, m, n, o, p, u, and w.

14. Sonora Louise Smart Dodd of _____ was the originator of Father's Day. It was first officially celebrated on June 19, 1910.

15. _____ was the birthplace of such notables as Robert Frost, John Steinbeck, Jack London, General George S. Patton, William Randolph Hearst, Joe DiMaggio, and Richard Nixon.

Pacific and Northwest States Map

Trivia Answers

East and Northeast

1. Connecticut
2. Vermont
3. Delaware
4. Maryland
5. New Jersey
6. Rhode Island
7. New York
8. Pennsylvania
9. Massachusetts
10. Rhode Island
11. Vermont
12. Maine
13. Massachusetts
14. New Hampshire
15. New Jersey

South and Southeast

1. Alabama
2. Arkansas
3. Georgia
4. Florida
5. Georgia
6. Louisiana
7. Tennessee
8. Kentucky
9. Louisiana
10. Mississippi
11. Virginia
12. Mississippi
13. North Carolina
14. South Carolina
15. West Virginia

Midwest

1. Wisconsin
2. South Dakota
3. Ohio
4. Missouri
5. Michigan
6. Iowa
7. Illinois
8. Indiana
9. Kansas
10. Minnesota
11. North Dakota
12. Oklahoma
13. Illinois
14. Nebraska
15. Oklahoma

Trivia Answers *(cont.)*

Southwest

1. Utah
2. Texas
3. Arizona
4. New Mexico
5. Texas
6. Nevada
7. Utah
8. Nevada
9. Texas
10. Utah
11. Arizona
12. New Mexico
13. Texas
14. Nevada
15. Utah

Mountain

1. Colorado
2. Wyoming
3. Idaho
4. Colorado
5. Montana
6. Wyoming
7. Montana
8. Idaho
9. Colorado
10. Montana
11. Montana
12. Wyoming
13. Colorado
14. Idaho

Pacific and Northwest

1. Washington
2. Hawaii
3. California
4. Alaska
5. California
6. Hawaii
7. Oregon
8. Oregon
9. Washington
10. Oregon
11. Alaska
12. California
13. Hawaii
14. Washington
15. California

How to Find Out More . . . on the Web

To access an Internet site to learn more about a topic, you will need a host address, such as the one shown. **http://www.tvpress.com/**

To view a site online, type in the address exactly as shown, with proper upper- and lowercase letters and all punctuation. If you have difficulty accessing a site, just type in the first part up to the type of organization. **com (commercial), edu (education), gov (government), org (nonprofit organization)**

World Wide Web sites are always changing. You may experience difficulty accessing a particular site. You might receive an error message like one of these:

- file not found
- server down
- cannot find server
- the home page has moved to another server
- the server or home page is no longer operating
- the server is busy

Receiving such an error message usually does not mean that you have done something wrong. Actually, it usually indicates a problem with the host server. In many instances, the server may not be up and running or may have already reached its quota of users. In this case, you should try a different time. Sometimes you can be successful in connecting if you try within five minutes after the error message.

Troubleshooting Web Addresses

1. Check your spelling. Remember that all addresses must be entered exactly as written.

2. Shorten the address so you have only the essential parts for the first home page.

3. Check to see if your keywords are appropriate for the information you are seeking.

4. Try some alternate sites.

How to Find Out More . . . on the Web (cont.)

Defining Your Search

Effective use of keywords is one way that you can define and narrow your search. A dialog box will allow you to type in a keyword or phrase.

The first step is to define the topic and type of information you want to find as specifically as possible.

Once you have identified the topic/content, you can choose appropriate keywords for your search. A diagram of this process is shown in the box.

Preparing for a Keyword Search

Define the topic:

    Identify the search objective:

    Choose a search engine or directory:

    Define the type of information as general or specific:

    Define your keywords:

    Keyword 1

    Keyword 2

    Keyword 3

    Keyword 4

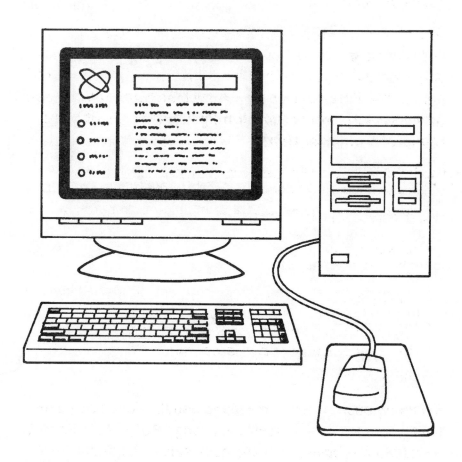

Before you begin an online search, list the keywords you intend to use. Include possible synonyms so they are handy if the keyword you used is nonproductive.

How to Find Out More . . . on the Web *(cont.)*

Northeast

http://www.massmaple.org/myo.html—This site gives detailed instructions on how to tap your own sugar maple with links to recipes.

http://fallscam.Niagara.com/—This site shows an interesting live view of Niagara Falls.

http://pilgrims.net/plimouthplantation/vtour/index.htm— Take a virtual tour of Plimouth Plantation at this Web site and see and learn how Pilgrims lived in the early days of our country.

http://www.hersheys.com/chocworld/main.html—You'll find a coloring book, puzzle, and a printable maze here—all related to chocolate.

South and Southeast

http://members.aol.com/Arrockinfo/pebblepups/pebblepuppies.html—Are you a budding rock hound? This site is for you—what to do with all those rocks! You'll find lots of Arkansas links here.

http://library.advanced.org/10320/peamunu.htm —More peanut butter recipes!

http://www.peanutbutterlovesr.com/Trivia/indix.htm/—Take a peanut butter quiz, and find out more about peanuts and peanut butter.

http://longwoo.cs.ucf.edu/~MidLink/native.discovery.html

—See kids' drawings of native animals in Florida. Submit drawings of native animals from your area to MidLink Magazine.

West, Southwest, Mountain

http://www.tpwd.state.tx.us/adv/kidspage/kidspage.htm— You'll find Texan wildlife, campfire stories, activities, coloring sheets, and more at this fun site.

http://members.aol.com/actanw/maps/clickable.html— Click on the map to see various parts of the Oregon Trail and what the pioneers had to say about it.

http://monhome.sw2.k12.us/west/brew/wildlife.html—This site has lots of photographs of Wyoming wildlife.

http://www2.cr.nps.gov/oad/adventure/landmarks/rock.htm —Print out a coloring sheet of Independence Rock.

http://www.ushistory.com/fight.htm—Listen to "Fight No More Forever," a song based on Chief Joseph's famous speech.

Pacific and Northwest

http://www.teelfamily.com/activities/snow/—Visit this Alaskan family's Web site and learn interesting things about snow—snow ice cream, an edible glacier, making snowflakes, growing a crystal snowflake, snow folk tales, and snow poems. Follow the links and view photos of Alaskan wildlife.

Index of Activities

Index of Activities (cont.)